P9-CAY-673

What people are saying about

pure genius

"Can school be a place where risk-taking and creativity flourish? Don Wettrick offers an emphatic 'Yes!'—and shows how he's done it. Wettrick has incorporated a range of creativity-generating concepts into his teaching and turned his classroom into an innovation factory. This book teaches you how to do the same and still maintain rigorous educational standards. You'll be amazed by his students' accomplishments and eager to put his ideas into practice."

—DANIEL PINK, author of *Drive* and *A Whole New Mind*

"Don Wettrick has turned the traditional classroom experience on its head, allowing the students to take control of their own education. The results are stunning! This book should be the blueprint for the future of education."

—TINA SEELIG, Professor, Stanford University, author of *inGenius*

"Don Wettrick has created a wonderful resource for bringing innovation down to earth and into the classroom. A valuable tool for educators!"

—TONY WAGNER, author of *Creating Innovators*

"Schools are failing our students and are in desperate need of a reboot. Don Wettrick provides compelling examples of innovative practices that create a culture of learning that is relevant and authentic. His book is a call to action to create an education system that inspires students to learn and provides skill sets that the real world demands."

—ERIC SHENINGER, author of *Digital Leadership*

"Level up your learning by understanding the pure genius of having one class dedicated to innovation, making, and the pursuit of student interests. Don Wettrick gives you the definitive guidebook on this transformational method of teaching and transforming school to a relevant place where students want to learn."

—VICKI DAVIS, author *Reinventing Writing*

"Don Wettrick is transforming the classroom experience. In this book, he opens the doors and freely shares how he's developed the innovative genius in so many people—and how you can do it too, whether you are a teacher, parent, or student."

—DAVE BURKUS, author of *The Myths of Creativity*

"Empower students and they will amaze you. I found Don Wettrick through one of his students who had created a DVD with the intention of teaching school administrators in Indiana why and how to use social media. It turned out that her teacher, Wettrick, enabled his students to work on innovations that made a difference to them and their community. I was impressed enough to ask Wettrick and his student to speak to my Stanford class, who were as amazed as I was. Wettrick is one of the hero teachers who isn't waiting for educational reform to innovate. He is innovating by supporting his own students' creative collaborations. Listen to him."

—HOWARD RHEINGOLD, Stanford University, author of *Net Smart*

"Pure Genius by Don Wettrick is a wonderful read that highlights ways to unlock creativity and the power for teachers and students to be innovative in the classroom. It's filled with anecdotes, examples, and actionable ideas for instant implementation."

—ADAM BELLOW, co-author of *Untangling the Web*

pure genius

Building a Culture of
INNOVATION
and Taking
20% TIME
to the Next Level

Don Wettrick

Pure Genius
© 2014 by Don Wettrick

All rights are reserved. No part of this publication may be reproduced in any form or by any electronic or mechanical means, including information storage and retrieval systems, without permission in writing by the publisher, except by a reviewer who may quote brief passages in a review. For information regarding permission, contact the publisher at daveburgessconsulting@gmail.com.

This book is available at special discounts when purchased in quantity for use as premiums, promotions, fundraising, and educational use. For inquiries and details, contact: daveburgessconsulting@gmail.com.

This publication is designed to provide accurate and authoritative information in regard to the subject matter covered. It is sold with the understanding that the publisher is not engaged in rendering legal, accounting, or other professional service. If legal advice or other expert assistance is required, the services of a competent professional person should be sought.

Published by Dave Burgess Consulting, Inc.
San Diego, CA
http://daveburgess.com

Edited by Erin K. Casey
Cover Design by Genesis Kohler
Interior Design by My Writers' Connection

Library of Congress Control Number: 2014948102
ISBN 13TP: 978-0-9882176-2-1
ISBN 13TP Ebook: 978-0-9882176-3-8
First Printing: September 2014

For Emma Wettrick, who exemplified compassion and love.

Contents

Acknowledgments ix

Foreword xi

Introduction 1

1 Why Innovate? 5

2 Creating a Culture
of Innovation & Leadership 17

3 There Is No Plan 29

4 Six Building Blocks of
Innovative Learning 45

5 Social Media & Teachers 59

6 Social Media & Students 77

7 Getting Started with Social Media 91

8 Opportunities Are Everywhere 105

9 Student Voices 117

10 Moving Forward 133

Coming Together:
Speaking the Same Language 145

Additional Resources 153

About the Author 155

Acknowledgments

Writing this book has been a joy, but I admit there were some sacrifices along the way. So the first person I want to acknowledge is my wife, Alicia. I want to thank you for "tutoring" me in ninth grade Algebra class in 1988, agreeing to date me a year later, and ultimately saying yes to a marriage proposal. I am completely honored to call you my wife, and I cherish all that you do for me and the family.

To my children Ava, Anna, and Grant: Thank you for being patient with your dad behind the computer. I tried hard to write most of this while you were sleeping, but my apologies if I went on too long. Words can't express how much you mean to me.

My first two teachers, Chuck and Sue Wettrick: You taught me integrity and unconditional love.

To my book advisors, especially Vicki Davis, Eric Sheninger, and Dave Burgess: Thank you! Vicki and Eric, you provided so much insight on what it took to write a book. Dave, you have been a mentor and friend throughout the entire process. I also want to thank Sherry Crofut, a friend and educator who made me write this book. Without your constant emails and texts asking for updates, I might not have finished.

To my former and current students: Your success and determination is what is being showcased. Learning how to be innovative together has made me a better educator, and more importantly, a lifelong learner.

To my first love in teaching, Greenwood Middle School: While I went on to pursue other interests in education, Greenwood has always been my home.

To the great people at Franklin High School: Your patience and willingness to take a chance is what helped start this educational journey.

To Noblesville High School: I am honored to teach at a school that has such a commitment to innovation and excellence.

To my editor and book coach, Erin Casey: Your skills as an editor exceeded my expectations. You are not only a great editor but also a voice of reason.

Publisher's Foreword

The world is in a constant state of change and forward progression. Unfortunately, our schools are one of the segments of society slowest to adapt to the demands of the changing marketplace. As such, too many of today's students are catapulted into an uncertain future, ill-equipped to deal with the challenges they will face.

We do our students a disservice when we prepare them for a world that no longer exists and fail to empower them with the skills and abilities they will need to navigate rough and shifting seas. We don't need students who can fill in bubbles on a multiple-choice test; we need students who can create, innovate, connect, and collaborate. We need students who can identify and solve complex, real-world problems. Changing the way we educate students is not only necessary…it's a moral imperative.

For far too long schools have been bastions of boredom, killers of creativity, and way too comfortable with compliance and conformity. The great challenge, of course, is how to create that change within a system so entrenched in its ways and invested in the status quo. Fortunately, I believe you are holding the answer. In *Pure Genius*, Don Wettrick provides a systematic blueprint for how to teach innovation in any school. This is not theory. Don walks the talk. He is an educator who speaks with authority because he has traversed the highs and lows of building an entirely new kind of class. He not only shares his vision for educational reform but also delivers a persuasive pitch as to why innovation can—and should—be part of any class at any level.

In my book, *Teach Like a PIRATE*, I professed that we need educators who are willing to sail into uncharted waters with no guarantee of success, willing to reject the status quo, and willing to have an entrepreneurial attitude towards reform. We need rebels, mavericks, and risk-takers who are willing to fly their flags in defiance and embrace unorthodox methods in the pursuit of educational treasure. Don Wettrick is a pirate, and *Pure Genius* is sure to recruit more to the crew.

It has been a great pleasure collaborating, creating, connecting, and innovating with Don to publish this book. I have had the honor to see the principles of his class come to life during the production of *Pure Genius*. I'm proud to publish this book under the Dave Burgess Consulting, Inc., label because I know that you are reading a book, a manifesto, with the power to transform school for kids.

Don Wettrick is an agent of change. More importantly, *Pure Genius* contains the secrets of how you can become an agent of change, as well, so you can equip your students for *their* futures, teach them to think for themselves, and empower them with a spirit of innovation. Welcome to the educational revolution.

Dave Burgess
President, Dave Burgess Consulting, Inc.
Author of *Teach Like a PIRATE*
daveburgess.com

pure genius

INTRODUCTION

Have you ever watched a movie that was so good, so mind-blowing that you left the theater and *never wanted to talk about it?* The last time you heard your favorite song on the radio, did you *turn it down?* Or when you ate at a new, amazing restaurant, did you *keep the experience to yourself?*

Of course not!

When we come across something awesome, we want to spread the word, turn it up, and talk about it. People love to share great experiences with each other. Just like the shirtless guy posing in the mirror for a selfie on Instagram—which, by the way, is *not* an effective or appropriate way to use social media—we want to share. We feel a sense of pride because we think we've discovered something amazing, and we love the camaraderie created when we share our discovery with like-minded people.

When I talk about our innovation experiment at the high school where I teach, I feel that same rush of pride and excitement. I am thrilled by the connections this class time fosters with other students and educators.

I started my first Innovation Class in 2012 after being inspired by Daniel Pink's TED talk, "The Puzzle of Motivation,"[1] and then reading his book, *Drive*. (I like his work so much that I have since read everything he has written, including his inspiring graphic novel, *Johnny Bunko*.) If you're unfamiliar with the term, an Innovation Class is one in which students can have time and space to create their own learning experiences and collaborate with experts from around the world. It is also a place where students learn by doing and creating, rather than passively listening to a set of directions and pre-determined outcomes. And although we make sure to meet our standards, the focus is less on compliance and more on self-discovery and the pursuit of curiosity and knowledge building.

Innovation accurately describes what goes on during this type of class. You may have also heard similar concepts described as *20% Time* or *Genius Hour, Google Time*, and *Maker Spaces*. I use the term *Innovation Class* because it's the label with which I am most comfortable. If you decide to try this experiment in your classroom, use whatever name you prefer—or innovate and make up your own label. I hope you will try it. In fact, one of my goals with this book is to show why our quest for innovation should not be reduced to one hour of the week. While I love a Genius Hour, I want to encourage more educators, students, and parents to sharpen their skills of innovation, expand their opportunities for collaboration, and learn how to amplify their message via social media—every day and in every class.

In the following pages, I'll share experiences and lessons I've learned from our Innovation Class. I'll also shed some light on how this approach has worked in other classrooms from elementary, middle, and high school levels. You'll read about other educators who are successfully using passion-based innovation time to challenge and prepare their students for life beyond the classroom. Throughout this book, I'll share why I believe these classes, or portions of class time, can provide insight and change the way we educate and equip our students.

In addition to my desire to share my own exciting discovery, I wanted to give students a voice and include them in the conversation about innovation. I have attended many conferences where "educational experts" present their thoughts on what educators should do. Unfortunately, many of those well-educated, self-proclaimed experts have never taught or even worked with children. I've read countless articles and reports about what today's students need, yet I don't read much from today's students. Shouldn't we want to hear from more students who are taking educational risks? Could their perspectives provide insight into what is and isn't working in classrooms today? I believe so. Thus, this book includes a few of the many lessons I've learned from my students. What you read here will help you understand how an innovative approach to learning has changed the lives of both teachers and students.

Don't get me wrong; our Innovation Class was not always so successful or life-changing. In fact, I've learned quite a bit about what *not* to do. The truth is, too much freedom and autonomy can create problems. Yet, I believe few classes, or schools, fail in such beautiful ways as an Innovation Class. That's why, in the process of learning, we celebrate failing. (I like to refer to our failures as *numerous prototypes*.) Failure teaches us to tweak the formula and create a better, more meaningful experience. By nature, innovation is always a work in progress.

What you won't find in *Pure Genius* is a bunch of educational jargon. Although I wrote this book with teachers in mind, I want as many people as possible to join in the discussion of educational change. I hope parents and students will read this and seek out the advantages of purposeful innovation and true collaboration. With this audience in mind, using phrases like across *cognitive and affective domain, bringing value-added learning, throughout multiple modalities*, or even acronyms like API (Academic Performance Index), AYP (Adequate Yearly Progress), or even NCLB (No Child Left Behind), might get in the way, or worse, seem too Ivory Tower and not down-to-earth enough.

To be truthful, I am not an educational expert; rather, I am a passionate educator who wants to bring about positive and meaningful change. I do not have all the answers to education. What I do have are insights on how to create moments of sheer joy in the classroom, and I want to pass along those experiences. My hope is that this book sparks some debate and opens a dialogue about how we can improve education today. I'd love to hear from you about what is and isn't working. I really want to connect with positive people who are willing to embrace change and take risks. I challenge us all to turn off that negative voice that says, "You can't." As you read this book, wonder, *What if....?* When a new idea sparks in your mind, share it with me on Facebook.com (don.wettrick) or on Twitter (@donwettrick), and let the dialogue begin!

Speaking of Facebook and Twitter, I hope this book inspires you to get involved and become active on social media. How and where we get information is changing. Education is moving in an exciting direction because of social media. Your students are learning and connecting online and that's where we educators can learn from each other in a bigger, better way.

[1] http://www.ted.com/talks/dan_pink_on_motivation

WHY INNOVATE?

What's the real problem with education today? If you asked fifty people that question, you'd get fifty different answers.

Numerous newspaper and television reports, as well as movie-length documentaries, have highlighted the under-performance of the American public school system. Each report and program offers a different perspective on the severity of the issues. It seems the one thing experts, as well as parents and teachers, agree on is that our education system needs a lot of work. Unfortunately, very few people offer feasible solutions. Instead, these experts and commentators freely place blame and debate opinions about the reasons for our schools' failures and how students' lives are affected. It seems that agreeing on the real problem is the hardest part, which is why it's where we must start.

Through trial and error in our Innovation Class, my students have learned that asking the right questions is one of the most important steps in problem solving. Before we can solve the problem, we have to define it. Questions help us do that.

So my question is: *Why do we need innovation in our schools?*

> **Innovation** uses a fresh approach to **solving real problems** with the resources you have and **finding clever ways around** the resources you don't have.

The word *innovation* gets thrown around without much explanation. Like the word *extreme* in the 1990s, innovation has been so overused it has lost its meaning. I recently watched a commercial for toilet paper that claimed a "new innovative layer of softness and absorption." Toilet paper. Innovative? I wince when I see this beautiful word become cliché.

Why innovation? How is innovation going to fix the problems that students and educators face today? The answer: Innovation brings new solutions to problems that arise in a changing environment.

Times have changed. The factory model of education—the one that educates students based on age groups in preparation for assembly line and office cubicle jobs—no longer works. Our current system doesn't address the demands of our changing economy and marketplace. How many jobs are available in factories? Compare that figure to the number of computer coding jobs that need to be filled. Then consider how many completely new job titles and roles will be created in the next five years. We've all heard the argument that the marketplace has changed, and still we are slow to correct our educational system so that it supports our society's current and future demands. It's a critical problem urgently needing a solution. A fresh approach *is needed now!*

Innovation breaks down barriers and introduces new, constantly evolving methods. It does *not* mean doing the same tasks with more money. Nor does it mean hoisting the school mission statement in a new italicized font on a banner in the foyer. Simply put, innovation uses a fresh approach to solving real problems with the resources you have and finding clever ways around the resources you don't have. And it requires a real understanding of the needs of your end users... *the students.*

Innovation Improves the Teaching Experience

Innovation starts at the teacher level. Teachers must be innovative in their approach to teaching, learning, and designing new experiences.

When he was about to retire from teaching, my father gave me some advice just before my first year of teaching: "Don, I don't care if you teach for the next twenty years; just don't teach one year twenty times." In other words, you can teach for twenty years; just don't *do the same thing* for twenty years.

The practical wisdom of his words didn't fully sink in until my third year of teaching. I saw some teachers use the same worksheets over and over, show the same films, and do the same field trips. Those teachers (luckily not that many) did this for years and years, while others moved on to other jobs because they were, I assume, bored.

So as I headed into my third year of teaching and every year since, I chose to start fresh. Now, each semester I select a few successes from the previous year to repeat, but I enjoy coming up with and trying new ideas. I challenge myself to pick up new skills that will make an impact on my students and feed my own curiosity. I am now in Year Seventeen of my journey of being a teacher, but I'm in Year Forty-Two of being a learner. I am just as curious as my students to embrace new challenges. I've learned to accept failure as a part of the journey, and I hope to never stop learning.

Luckily, I have the privilege of teaching classes that will never stop evolving. It is impossible to keep up with all the newest software, updates, gadgets, and changes in technology... and I love this. I have learned that it is okay to learn along with the students, and, in many cases, learn from them! I *want* to stay relevant, and, if that means that I start new every year, I accept the challenge.

Innovation Makes Learning Fun and Relevant

When teachers make material applicable to their everyday lives, students can see the value of learning and how our classes are relevant. If a student asks, "Why are we learning this stuff?" and the only answer the teacher can come up with is, "Because it's on the test," it's time to innovate. Conversely, a classroom that is producing meaningful, relevant content will not only win the hearts and minds of the students but will also push the students to look for more opportunities to use newly learned techniques.

I mentioned that my content evolves naturally because technology is constantly changing, but what about non-tech classes? Can a standard math or language class innovate from one year to another? The answer is "Yes!" Take a popular game like *Minecraft* and start looking for teachable math lessons. Explore the possibilities of *Dragon Box*, an electronic game that teaches the basics of algebra. English classes are now more relevant than ever due to the popularity of blogging. Collaborative writing tools are a way for our students to make the shift from being consumers to content-originators by producing eBooks, or learning how to self-publish a class novel. (I highly encourage English teachers to take a look at Vicki Davis's book, *Reinventing Writing*, in which she details a new, modern approach to writing.)

Regardless of the subject, relevancy is the biggest key to retention. A commitment to innovation helps keep students engaged because they can see how the material and methods can improve or affect their lives.

Innovation Makes the Most of "The System"

Later in this book, I provide specific examples of good and bad Innovation Class experiences that others and I have had along the way. Before we get there, however, I must address the most frequent question I get about the Innovation Class concept. It isn't about how we spend our time in the classroom or what the students work on. It is about meeting Common Core State Standards.

Let me be clear: The purpose of this book is *not* to hash out the good or bad qualities of the Common Core initiative. That subject can be and has been debated and argued elsewhere. I am not a policy maker; I am a teacher who chooses to work creatively within the constraints of the current system.

What's interesting is that I have talked with innovation converts who *hate* the common core as well as with those who love it. Both camps like

*Done right, innovation can **work with the Common Core AND allow freedom** in the teacher's approach as well as in the students' learning choices.*

this innovative approach to learning. Here's the key: Students are asked to take ownership of their education. Instead of teachers putting a standard on the board and telling them how to meet it, students are given the challenge to prove they have mastered the required standards. They are also given the freedom to choose the method for completing the projects they choose.

This model totally flips the classroom management style. Students are put in charge of their learning; the teacher remains available for support, guidance, or assistance. In my classroom, I literally work for the *students*, and they bring value to the class. My job is to help them achieve their goals, rather than have the students work for me. I'm there to help facilitate learning, help manage projects, and make connections.

Because we're operating within the system and still meeting the required standards, this model can work well with an administration that wants to try something different but is hesitant to go too extreme. Done right, innovation can work with the Common Core and allow freedom in the teacher's approach as well as in the students' learning choices.

An even bigger shift will occur when colleges begin to see the value of innovation and change, rather than focusing exclusively on the standard path toward higher learning.

Innovation Demands that Higher Education Evolve

Convincing students to take risks in school is a difficult task. To them, getting a good grade often seems more important than learning something new and interesting. Some students have told me they wouldn't take my class because it isn't weighted and thus wouldn't raise their GPA even if they received an A as a grade. In contrast, Advanced Placement (AP) courses fill up quickly because students know that colleges and universities look favorably on those advanced classes. When I ask students why they are taking an AP class, they respond that they feel they have to so they can get ahead.

Frankly, I don't blame the students. They are playing the game in which the rules rely on compliance. In the old way of taking classes, The System suggested *preferred* classes, rather than pursuing classes based on *personal passion and interests*. Going for the grade, obtaining high, standardized test scores, and seeking other filler classes for a decent college résumé are the hoops they jump through. I'm not making fun of students who list being on the chess club or organizing the homecoming dance on their college applications. If they are excited about those activities, great! But when students do these activities or take extra AP classes, not out of choice, but out of fear, there's a problem with the system. Students shouldn't fear that their dream college will pass them over if they don't take all the preferred courses.

> *Universities need to **reward risk takers** and **innovators** over grade chasers.*

Our universities need to reward risk takers and innovators over grade chasers. College admissions officers need to re-examine the value of the high Grade Point Average (GPA) and consider it against the initiative of students who pursue entrepreneurial interests. Take a second look at the students who chose to take an internship over a class with a weighted grade. Without help from the universities, convincing students to take creative risks will never happen. Students know how to play the game, and the current game doesn't reward creativity, choice, or risk.

Innovation Addresses the Real Problem

In the fall of 2013, I traveled to Google headquarters in Mountainview, California, with some of my students. While there, we talked to several employees about the qualities Google looks for in an employee. Without hesitation most of them identified creativity, entrepreneurship, and innovation as the top three traits. However, some acknowledged that the company was having a hard time finding enough employees from the United States. We found that many of Google's great programmers are from foreign countries. While there are certainly good coders from the United States working at Google, many of them were mostly self-taught and did not have the same access to computer science classes in high school as did their co-workers from other countries.

Most people acknowledge that not enough computer sciences courses are offered in the United States. As a result, jobs are going unfilled or are being filled by people from outside the country. And still our system is slow to change.

Innovation Isn't About Money

Some parents and teachers believe that, with more funds, our schools will do better. The truth is, while educational dollars spent in the United States have increased through the years, the results haven't improved to reflect increased funding. And currently, our sluggish economy and forced cutbacks are creating new problems. The economic realities are that more funding might not happen for a while. The money just isn't there.

Nor Is It About Change for the Sake of Change

Some politicians call for sweeping changes and standardized tests. It's no wonder teachers are already skeptical of change for the sake of change. I don't blame them. The educational-philosophy-of-the-day mentality has left many educators exhausted and confused. Thus, when we talk about need to change education, many teachers think, *When* aren't *we changing?*

So, we have an existing problem—a need for sweeping educational change at the primary, secondary and university levels—with new variables: less money, fewer jobs, lower property taxes, and lower opinion ratings on our schools. For education to get out of this rut, we must be more—you guessed it—*innovative*. And not the overused term of toilet paper technology, but truly innovative.

COLLABORATION: The Name of the New Game

I attended Microsoft's Innovative Educator Forum in 2011 and was dumbfounded when the Vice President of Microsoft Education, Anthony Salcito, opened his keynote speech to teachers with, "Students are learning without us." Quietness filled the room. After a long dramatic pause, he continued to explain that the web is filling in the gaps with video tutorials, wikis, games, and online tutors.

Before the teachers could run for the exits, he cautioned that online learning is indeed growing, but students still need to be together. I thought this was going to be the obvious lecture on how students need to socialize, get along with each other, attend prom, etc. However, he went another route and focused on collaboration.

I'll come back to this topic later in the book, but collaboration is at the heart of why we need an Innovation Class model. There is a certain magic in the air when students get together and work on things they are passionate about. Yes, students can sit at home and learn on their own, but together they're more dynamic and enthusiastic. When that enthusiasm runs over, students can change the world.

Foo Fighters and Video Games

I recently came across a quote from Dave Grohl, Foo Fighters' frontman and former drummer for the 90s band, Nirvana. He was talking about how the music industry has changed, and how making modern music is recording one track into a computer, then fixing everything on some software. Or worse yet, music is created by people performing on TV shows, singing songs they didn't create. Grohl went on to point out—I'm paraphrasing here—that to get better as a musician you have to get together with your band and play (collaborate) and fail. He understands that, to be great, you first must fail. You play (horribly), and play, and play for the sheer passion of it. Then, if and when your passion is discovered by the masses, it is authentic because it has developed organically.

I love Grohl's insights here. Starting out, you'll have inferior equipment, a lack of talent, no real audience, and people telling you that you aren't going to make it. Sound familiar? Lack of funds? Lack of support? Low test scores? Being judged by failure?

Yet pursuing anything valuable or important means you *have to be willing to fail*. Ask a student if he would ever recommend a video game that he completely won on his first life. Watch the sheer joy of a player who fails

*Pursuing anything valuable or important means you have to be willing to **fail**.*

13

and then presses reset. He loves it. He wants to go right back to the obstacle and beat it! He loses again and again and keeps coming back. Why? Because he has hope. Because he works at his own pace. There are no labels, and, when he succeeds, there is immediate feedback by a real audience, not just a grade.

Can you imagine teaching a video game in class the traditional way?

TEACHER: "Hello class, please go to level one on your game console."

STUDENT: "But Mr. Wettrick, I already have prior experience with this game, I'm on level twenty-two," cries a student.

TEACHER: "No! Everyone must start on level one. We are a class and we work at the same pace."

STUDENT: "But I've already mastered these levels two months ago. I don't want to do it again."

You get the point. But, what if we were to empower the advanced student to work with other gamers to find solutions together? Or try to collaborate with the game designer in California to write a beta test for another level? Or just allow him/her to help the other students to get to his/her level faster?

The reason I shared Dave Grohl's vision of music and the video game analogies is to point out that *constraints lead to creativity*. Working around bad equipment is a blessing. Having everything you want is a curse. The right thing to do is empower those students who are on another level to keep moving forward, instead of sitting there being an A student.

In addition to the Innovation Class, I taught a variety of high school broadcasting classes in the past. Cameras, lighting, sound and video editing equipment are extremely expensive. Constant updates and changing technology mean that there is always a new camera, software updates, or fancy new grip equipment available. I *never* had enough money to fulfill my students' unlimited wants (notice I didn't say *needs*). In my experience, working around what we didn't have made for a much better learning opportunity. The constraints of limited equipment and technology forced students to get creative to make their projects look professional. Blaming the equipment is not an option. If a video didn't come out the way they'd hope, we did more research, more experimentation, and tried more innovative techniques. From there we empowered advanced students to keep pushing themselves to go even further. They, in turn, inspired the rest of the class to get to their level.

Side note: To help make up what our budget lacked, we watched for opportunities to shoot commercials and found contests that paid cash. These allowed students to work hard with the available equipment to earn better gear. Plus, equipment *earned* by the students is treated better than equipment that was *provided* by the school.

In short, innovation in education *is* education. You can and should be innovative in *any* classroom, whether you have a chunk of time called Genius Hour, or just a willingness to integrate new approaches to learning.

This book, *Pure Genius*, doesn't contain a specific set of directions or strategies for convincing your administration to approve an Innovation Class. Instead, let's make do with what we have. Accept some of the realities of our classrooms and challenge our students to make the situation better. I want my students to be more like *MacGyver*. Remember that TV show? That guy could stop a bomb from going off with only the resources he had on hand. Using a wad of bubble gum, the foil wrapper, and a thread off his jacket, he could stymie a terrorist. We need attitudes like MacGyver's to combat lackluster education.

Having a fun, new school curriculum is exciting. Knowing the answers ahead of time is boring. Going through a class without failing at all is not a challenge, and, thus, not very rewarding. Yes, students like to boast that they got an A on the test, but do they value the grade if they exert very little effort and still received an A? So, let's provide them with experiences to grow by collaborating, creating a culture of positive failure, and allowing them the freedom to research and pursue what is important to them.

This is what the Innovation Class model is all about.

quick thoughts

- Education needs action, not rhetoric.
- Online learning is growing, but student collaboration remains vital.
- A lack of resources can be a blessing if you find creative ways around the problem.
- Real world projects can be solved if we give students time and resources.

notes

CREATING A CULTURE OF INNOVATION & LEADERSHIP

The email I received from a trusted friend and mentor teacher simply read: "Watch it. Now!" I clicked the YouTube link, and my world changed.

Okay. It may not have been as dramatic as that, but almost.

The link led to Daniel Pink's TED (Technology Entertainment Design) talk. What I learned in those nineteen minutes, and through subsequent years of study and classroom experiments, has made, and continues to make, an incredible and positive impact on my students and me. If you have not watched this video, I highly encourage you to watch it. *Now.* Seriously. Put down this book and type into your browser's search bar: Daniel Pink and The Puzzle of Motivation.

Pink's TED talk discusses brain research that reveals how motivation factors, such as money, are out of balance. He surmises that, although money is an effective incentive when people are working on lower-level tasks like stacking boxes, financial rewards are actually counterproductive when it comes to higher-level thinking. He also offers examples of companies that have successfully broken out of the money/stock option model of motivation to use techniques such as results only work environment (ROWE) and 20% Time. The latter incentives allow for freedom and mastery. These innovative companies found that, by giving employees the freedom to work on subjects they find interesting and providing some resources, their job satisfaction increases significantly. More importantly, as Google discovered, inquisitive and satisfied employees often come up with interesting data and solutions during their free time. In fact, Google has admitted that many of its advancements resulted when employees were allowed the freedom to focus on their passions.

Pink also points out the differences of Microsoft's Encyclopedia Encarta vs. Wikipedia. Encarta provided financial incentives to experts who compiled a massive electronic encyclopedia. Wikipedia provided no financial incentives, but encouraged open collaboration. Open collaboration and freedom won out over financial rewards paid to professional authors. Microsoft discontinued Encarta in 2009. In contrast, Wikipedia is still going and expanding.

While Pink's presentation focused on business, it struck a chord with educators all over the world. His short speech blew me away! I showed it to my students the very next period. After watching, we discussed whether the average high school student could handle an open class. Some students laughed it off; others were amazed. A few were annoyed that they couldn't have such a class right then and there! I shared their frustration.

The concept of freedom and mastery made so much sense; I knew I *had* to create a class that would provide this type of environment for my students. Getting administrative buy-in and approval for an entire class period would take time. That reality existed far in the future. Rather than wait, I decided to create my own 20% Time in my Language Arts class right away. Enthusiastic and optimistic about the new idea, the students and I planned out the class the next day. We determined that on Fridays, students would research something about which they were passionate. The following week, they would use their 20% Time to blog about their findings and/or make a one-minute presentation.

In the course of planning I asked, "If I gave you an hour every Friday to explore any topic—something you've wanted to know more about, but never had the time to study—what would you work on or research?"

A sparkle in their eyes energized the room. Phrases like, "Finally, a class that is cool," and "Man, I'm going to learn about stuff that I want to learn," floated through the room. I encouraged them to find inspiration from apps like Stumbleupon.com and Reddit.com, as well as magazines and websites. We felt so much enthusiasm and were excited by the possibilities!

*When my students suddenly had the **freedom** to learn whatever they wanted, they **didn't know what to do**.*

Then utter disappointment and sheer terror struck.

That first Friday, student after distressed student said, "I don't know what I'm passionate about." "I don't know what I'm interested in." A handful of students jumped in right away, surfing sites that appealed to them, watching tutorials, reading blogs, etc., but most stared blankly at the screen. Some students even asked me to recommend a topic. A few feared they would fail the assignment because they didn't know what really interested them.

Freedom Is Hard

Hearing them complain, I remembered an experience from the summer before. I had met a man named Arthur at a soup kitchen where my wife and I serve once a month. He circulated through the crowd frantically asking everyone for money—not to pay for housing or food… he needed money to pay his parole fees. (I didn't even know such fees existed.) The paradox: Arthur *wanted* to work, but his felony record limited his options. Worse, if he couldn't pay the fees he would end up back in jail.

After spending an hour with him, I believed his sincerity. He knew he had made some terrible mistakes. He matured in prison, and he just wanted to be a normal, productive citizen. What he discovered, however, is what my students were complaining about: Freedom is hard. Being told what to do, although not exciting, is easy.

To earn the money he needed for the parole fee, Arthur helped me paint my house the following week. I learned so much by spending a day with this man whose perspective on life was totally different from my own. His admission about the difficulty of freedom struck a chord with me; his fundamentally simple message rang true. Arthur felt overwhelmed by the challenge of being out of prison. In jail, his meals were provided and he had no bills to pay or errands to run. Someone told him when to go to bed and what jobs to accomplish each day. Now that he was free, he had to find a job, but no one wanted to hire a felon with a violent history (in a bad economy, no less). The thought of wading through all the paperwork he had to complete to get assistance brought on panic attacks. To sleep at night, he locked himself into his very small bedroom in a group home; open space intimidated him. Confinement felt familiar and comfortable. Making his own decisions proved much tougher.

Not unlike Arthur, when my students suddenly had the freedom to learn whatever they wanted, they didn't know what to do. They were not accustomed to making their own learning choices and doing so felt daunting. The problem is that we've long viewed freedom as an option for idle time and/or laziness rather than productivity and exploration. As a result, students often believe they have only two options: Do what I'm told, or do nothing at all.

> **Freedom is hard.** *Being told what to do, although not exciting, is easy.*

I learned from that initial experience that 20% Time wasn't a magic cure. Interestingly, about 20 percent of the students to which I introduced 20% Time valued it. The other 80 percent imploded. We kept trying for two months, then, mercifully, the summer break arrived. Despite the struggle and frustration of that two-month experiment, the insights and knowledge gained within the small group inspired me to push on and write a description for a totally new class.

Now, at this point, I have to acknowledge that the perfect circumstances aligned to make my dream class a reality. I worked in a public school with an administration that wasn't afraid to take risks. Before asking my principal, Craig McCaffrey, if I could offer the class the next year, I asked him to watch the TED talk. I wanted him to get excited about the idea. It worked... sort of.

He chuckled and said, "Sure, but what are you going to call it? I don't see a Daniel Pink class on the state approved course catalogue." But I took his question as a good sign since he wasn't shutting the door on the idea. I pushed on, quoting a line from the movie *Dumb and Dumber*, "So, you're telling me there's a chance." (It probably helped that Craig had just accepted a school leadership position at another school; therefore, I reasoned, my request had a greater chance of being accepted because he would not be there the next year anyway.)

First things first, I had to figure out where my new class could fit into the state's course catalogue. One course title was just vague enough in nature that I thought I could make it my own. It was called Group Discussions. The description stated that students would be able to formulate topics, hold discussions in a group, and then write about their conclusions. I built on that open-ended definition and took my newly crafted course description back to my principal. He approved it, as did the school board. Then the real work began.

I knew the course had to be successful in its trial year; otherwise, the first class might also be the last. I knew, too, that the initial class would set the tone for future classes. Remembering that only a small percentage of the students knew how to deal with freedom, I wrote an application for prospective students. I took nominations from other teachers and interviewed the candidates. Early on, I realized that creating the right culture is a crucial factor for an Innovation Class or even 20% Time. That's why, before we go into the nuts and bolts of an Innovation Class, I want to talk about establishing a culture of innovation and leadership.

Creating Culture of Freedom from Day One

My mission on the first day of school is to create a culture. Rather than giving students a list of things they cannot do, my goal is to excite them about the possibilities of the coming year. *Nobody* gets excited about what they cannot do; it's human nature to oppose rules and regulations. Let me explain.

Think about the television commercials you see. The legal stuff (the product's limitations or potential side effects) is presented *after* the good stuff (the benefits of buying it). Prescription drug advertisements are a good example. The ad usually starts by giving you a glimpse of how your life can be better with the new medicine. Once you're convinced, the maker lists all the dire health warnings. Car commercials hype up the low payments or attractive lease rates before giving you the bottom line. If you're a *Saturday Night Live* fan, you might remember the "Happy Fun Ball" mock commercial where the kids first pitch the product, then the ad goes into ninety seconds of disclaimers, including, "Happy Fun Ball can accelerate to dangerous speeds," and "Do not taunt Happy Fun Ball."

I bring up disclaimers because the typical protocol for the first day of school is to focus on rules and regulations. When students come in, they are excited to see all their friends, show off their new outfits, and try out all their new supplies. Do you seriously think they want to hear an hour's worth of things they *cannot* do? No. They want to be inspired! The first impression of your class is so important.

When you lead with rules and regulations on the first day, you set a culture of limitations. Even if it isn't your intention, it is the reality. The mood immediately shifts from wonderment to negativity. Creativity is lost and hopes are dashed.

Students want to go home and enthusiastically tell their parents about their new classes. They are excited by possibilities, not limitations. Thus, I try to supply a little of what we all yearn for: hope. From the first day, I let my students know that the Innovation Class is designed to allow risk. I explain that they will be allowed to take chances, fail, and then succeed. I love telling stories to illustrate how their journeys might play out. Maybe it's a story of how my daughter Anna learned to walk, or, perhaps, it's a story about my hardest college class. My goal is to let them know that trial and error processes are welcomed here.

Lead with the exciting possibilities for your class rather than a list of what students can't do.

My high school students quickly grasp the concept of failing as a part of learning. That said, some teachers won't feel comfortable saying, "We're all gonna fail!" to set the tone for their class. That's okay. Find the key concept for your class. Maybe it's compassion, the love of learning, or curiosity. Whatever your theme is, lead with the exciting possibilities for your class rather than a list of what students can't do. Set a positive, hopeful tone for the rest of the year… your class journey.

Even after it's established that risk and failure are acceptable, even desirable, it takes time for students to adjust to freedom. Just as I experienced in my two-month experiment, several teachers have shared with me that they were dumbfounded when students sat waiting for instructions on what project or passion they should choose to work on during Genius Hour. In the first year of my Innovation Class, two students with high grade point averages asked me, "Would you just assign me a project, or have me write a research paper, or something?" The freedom to pursue projects and choose what they wanted to learn proved stressful for many of my students. Put simply, it is easier and less stressful to be told what to do, rather than be given freedom to come up with what you want to learn.

Sadly, our education system hasn't equipped students to think on their own. As Howard Rheingold, a noted author and adjunct professor at Stanford University, explained to me, "Students are excellent at figuring out what is going to be on the test, but have not had much practice in inquiring on their own, in thinking critically about the material and

> *One of the most **critical** components of teaching is helping students **find** **their passion**— their bliss.*

expressing themselves publicly about their critical thinking."

To get past the freedom paradox, devote ample time during the first two weeks of school to brainstorming possibilities. Help your students see freedom as liberating, rather than daunting. One of the most critical components of teaching is helping students find their passion—their bliss. Joseph Campbell, a noted, world mythology expert known for inspiring George Lucas to write *Star Wars*, explains the power of discovering and following your passion:

"If you do follow your bliss you put yourself on a kind of track that has been there all the while, waiting for you, and the life that you ought to be living is the one you are living. Follow your bliss and don't be afraid, and doors will open where you didn't know they were going to be."

Helping students truly find their bliss is one of the greatest gifts we can give. If you are a teacher, you might have received The Letter. Sometimes it's written at the end of the school year, other times, years past graduation, but The Letter usually gives thanks. The most inspiring letters I've received express gratitude for helping students find their passions. Often that discovery comes during a discussion at the beginning of the year when we were working on creating our class culture. Establishing a positive expectation of freedom challenges students to find their bliss.

Creating a Culture of Leadership

Coach Mike Krzyzewski (Coach K) exemplifies success in college basketball. He has taken Duke University to the national title games eight times and won four championships. While winning is exciting, I'm most impressed with his ability to foster a positive team culture.

Coach K has established a culture of success at Duke. They win... period. Why do they win so often? Because they focus on fundamentals, academics, and personal growth. Coach K sets his expectations on developing players into great leaders, not just NBA talent.

Herb Dove, a close friend of mine, played at Purdue University in the early 1990s. When I asked him about playing against Duke, he said, "Duke doesn't have the best athletes in basketball. They have the smartest, best athletes in basketball. Duke players know they have to hit the books and play hard." Dove carried a 3.85 GPA and respected the Blue Devil players. His insight was not born out of jealousy, but rather from his admiration for the program.

Success breeds success. With high expectations on and off the court, Coach K has created a culture of hard work, dedication, determination, and winning. And it's a culture that produces leaders, not followers.

Creating leaders in our schools, as with sports teams, also starts with the culture. But how do you define leadership in the classroom? What does it mean to be a leader or a follower? And what happens when student leadership morphs into dictatorship? NFL legends Peyton Manning and Terrell Owens show us the dividing the line between being a leader and a being a tyrant.

PEYTON MANNING VS. TERRELL OWENS: A STUDY IN LEADERSHIP

Leaders should create more leaders, plain and simple. Great leaders do not lead a bunch of followers; rather, they lead to enable more responsibility and trust within the group. That way, they can take advantage of new opportunities while trusting that the leaders they've developed have the character and skill to take the reins and move forward.

Too many times, students (and adults) feel the opiate of power and start pushing people around. We all know what happens next: The group resents the poor treatment and the leader ends up with no one to lead.

> By **developing leaders** who in turn develop leaders, you can create a **culture of success**.

Another problem created by power is a lack of humility. Some leaders are eager to take all the credit for success. Even when the leader does the majority of the work, teammates don't like it when all the credit goes to one person. If success comes, it is usually short-lived because the people who made the success possible aren't allowed to share in its joy. Eventually, they leave. Denver Bronco quarterback, Peyton Manning, knows the importance of sharing the spotlight. Rather than spiking the ball and doing a touchdown dance, he gives credit to his teammates after a scoring drive. In post-game press conferences, he usually acknowledges his offensive line, receivers, coaches, and even the opponents. Rarely does he say, "Yeah, I was pretty great." Instead, he wants the players around him to be better, experience the praise, and grow as players.

Student leadership requires the same attitude, and it is up to the teachers to model this behavior. Show them that delegating responsibility and sharing the accolades is essential for a great team culture. Teaching them to share in the work and the praise equips student leaders to create more leaders. They learn to hand over their power to move forward, knowing that the group will succeed.

Likewise, they learn that humility can sustain their leadership. The shelf life of an egomaniac is a short one. People love the humble expert; they are relatable, yet revered at the same time. When a tyrant runs out of skill (or luck), people are just waiting to pounce. How often have you seen the build-them-up-and-tear-them-down mentality play out in the media? Interestingly, the media tends to seek out and destroy arrogant celebrities—the people whom the public wants to see go down in flames.

Looking at the sports metaphor again, think about Terrell Owens (aka T.O.). T.O. was a great receiver who possessed plenty of talent, but his teammates didn't want to work with him. When T.O. scored a touchdown he made sure everyone knew it; if he didn't score, it must have been the quarterback's fault. Compare that to Jerry Rice who put his focus on winning for the team. Even though he probably played two years past his prime, no one wanted Rice to leave; he was too valuable a leader in the locker room. One athlete created animosity and drama; the other shared responsibility and credit.

I hope you're excited about developing the next Peyton and Jerry and equally enthusiastic about coaching up the T.O. in your classroom. Fostering future leaders is the key to student success because good student leadership is inspiring and infectious. They can propel your entire school forward. By developing leaders who, in turn, develop leaders, you can create a culture of success.

quick thoughts

- Freedom leads to greater mastery.

- Freedom, however, is a cultural shift from what the students are used to.

- Set the culture of freedom and an acceptance of failure in the first two weeks of school.

- Create leaders by creating more leaders.
  Never dictate.

- Humility leads to sustainability and builds morale, rather than bitter followers.

notes

3

THERE IS NO PLAN

In Daniel Pink's graphic novel, *The Adventures of Johnny Bunko*, Diana, the genie, teaches Johnny how to make it in The Real World. The catch: She only imparts her knowledge *after* Johnny makes mistakes. (Perhaps experience is the best teacher.) One of the best lessons from the book is: There is no plan.

Trial and error, or implementing and adapting, is the name of the game when attempting a messy experiment like an Innovation Class. The motto, *There is no plan*, seems to fit. Success comes when you learn to adapt and *innovate*!

Before I go into the non-plan of this model's day-to-day operation, let me first explain what an Innovation Class is *not*. It is not a day off *for* your students, nor a day off *from* your students. I have heard numerous horror stories about teachers who mistakenly believed a Genius Hour equated to total freedom for students, during which time, the teachers, too, were free to grade papers or update their Facebook pages. Not surprisingly, these teachers felt stressed out or discouraged because their students didn't do anything and failed to live up to expectations.

The misconception that an Innovation Class is a free period for the teacher is way off. Quite the opposite is true; an Innovation Class demands more of the teacher's classroom time. Managing student projects and helping them find mentors requires a big commitment of time.

The Blueprint for an Innovation Class

Now that you know what not to expect (complete and total free time), let's take a look at the basic blueprint for an Innovation Class. While there is no plan, guidelines are a must.

- This is a project-based, passion-based course.
- Students research a topic of their personal interest.
- Students can work individually or in a group of up to three.
- Students must collaborate with an outside expert to gain knowledge and experience.
- Student must submit a project proposal with the standards, a timeline, and an approximate, fair point value.
- Students must blog/vlog (video blog) about their results weekly during class.
- Students present their projects to key stakeholders, turn in a reflection, and negotiate for their grade.

THIS IS A PROJECT-BASED, PASSION-BASED COURSE.

The student's freedom to choose a passion or topic of interest for the course is essentially the difference between an Innovation Class model and a problem-based learning (PBL) project for which the teacher assigns a project for the group. One of the key benefits of a passion-based project is that students learn how to love learning. Let me restate that… *Students learn how to love learning and embrace the quest for new opportunities!*

As I mentioned earlier, a stumbling block right out of the gate is that many students do not know what they are passionate about. For years, students have been told what topics to study and how to study them. Identifying a focus can be difficult. When students suddenly have the freedom and responsibility of discovering what they are passionate about, many of them are initially terrified. For this reason, we start most Mondays with a brainstorming session. This collaborative time allows the students to discover what their interest is

*One of the key benefits of a passion-based project is that **students learn how to love learning**.*

by throwing out ideas, hearing other students' thoughts, and adding to the discussion. Brainstorming days are among my favorite. These are days when students experience light-bulb moments, and I enjoy the pleasure of seeing their expressions when they discover a project's potential. The discovery process combined with the results of this creative practice is truly transformative.

Brainstorming is incredibly valuable to the class—and to life. If you're really interested in cultivating creativity, study techniques for brainstorming. It isn't just about sitting in a circle and tossing out ideas. That's what I did until I started researching how to brainstorm effectively in a group setting. For guidance, I highly recommend reading *inGenius* by Tina Seelig and *Creative Confidence* by Tom and David Kelly of IDEO. (For that matter, look into the company, IDEO, if you want to see creativity in action.)

STUDENTS RESEARCH A TOPIC OF PERSONAL INTEREST.

After identifying a topic that inspires them, students are tasked with researching the problem as well as possible solutions. They are challenged to look for the root causes of the need for change and to express why innovation is necessary or desirable.

I've found that it's preferable for the topic of choice to be something that needs improvement within their school or community. Students like to feel as if they can do something to resolve a problem. That said, a massive topic, like End World Hunger, ends up feeling overwhelming and discouraging. It's like writing a research paper on the topic of baseball. It's too broad a subject: spanning the history of the game, rules, records, players, etc. A narrower, more manageable focus for a paper might be Pete Rose. Encourage students to choose a focused topic for their project. Local needs or subjects are ideal; although, one can still think global and act local.

Students work individually or in a group of up to three.

Often, students choose to work in groups. Our most popular group size is two with a few groups of three. I do not allow groups of four or more. Experience has taught me that groups of four allow one member to coast while the others do all the work. Not surprisingly, that member's lack of effort can lead to some nasty disagreements. To avoid such conflict, I limit the group size and have the teams assign roles from the beginning. Every member should research and communicate with mentors, but some roles could include:

- Typing the proposal and final report.
- Tweeting and blogging about the project.
- Producing a PowerPoint, Prezi, or Keynote presentation.

Assigning specialist roles allows all team members to understand who is working harder and who needs to contribute more.

Students must collaborate with an outside expert to gain knowledge and experience.

Finding appropriate mentors/collaborators for projects often seems like a hurdle for students. That's true, at least in part, because I have high expectations. The first rule is: It can't be a parent. I want students to find mentors who are really experts, not just a nice neighbor or agreeable aunt. The downside of seeking out actual experts is that these professionals don't always have time to work or communicate with the students. Parents and family friends, on the other hand, are generally willing to make time.

Students can find mentors by reading magazines, listening to podcasts, and watching relevant television programs or newscasts. Understanding limitations on celebrities' and executives' time, students learn to identify ideal mentors. For example, whereas asking Peyton Manning to collaborate on a project regarding sports injuries might not be realistic, a surgeon from a local hospital might be a good fit.

I never discourage students from asking to contact an A-List collaborator, but I do give them a tight deadline. If a group wants to connect with Brad Pitt to collaborate on foreign adoptions, I give them three to four days to get a response. There is nothing wrong with shooting for the stars. Some of my students have connected with people I never thought would agree to work on school projects. In fact, many mentors are impressed when the students tell them what the class is and what they are trying to accomplish.

The biggest problem is with what I call wedding reception talk. Wedding reception talk is what happens when you strike up a conversation with an old friend or acquaintance. The chat turns nostalgic and inevitably one of you says, "We need to go out for a beer sometime," or "We should get together soon." You know right then and there it won't happen because you're both too busy, but it seems like the nice thing to say. Wedding reception talk comes

*Working with and getting to know **community leaders** and **influencers** is a **huge advantage for students.***

> *The **contacts** my students make during this class **help them stand apart** for **jobs, college acceptance**, and **scholarships**.*

easily for mentors. They don't want to disappoint the students by saying, "I'm too busy for your project." Instead they say, "We should do this sometime," but that sometime never comes. Requiring students to get a firm commitment from their mentors prevents them from wasting too much time waiting or trying to track them down later. Weeks of progress can be lost due to an unresponsive mentor, so it is important for a mentor to understand that the group's grade depends on his or her cooperation. I have even had a group require a signed agreement stating which days the mentor would be available to talk via phone or Skype.

Side note: Not all educators require mentors for their students' projects, but I believe collaborators are an essential part of a great Innovation Class experience. First, I don't have to be the expert on every topic. Second, and more importantly, the mentors are frequently key stakeholders in society. The potential for future employment or a strong reference is on the line! We all know the truth behind the phrase, "It's not what you know, but who you know." Working with and getting to know community leaders and influencers is a *huge* advantage for students. The contacts my students make during this class help them stand apart for jobs, college acceptance, and scholarships. For this reason alone, I believe teachers should require students to find mentors.

STUDENTS MUST SUBMIT A PROJECT PROPOSAL.

A project proposal is essentially a roadmap for and a hypothesis of the project. Additionally, it keeps students committed to a deadline. Each proposal's components differ, but these basics should be included:

- A driving question or problem that needs innovation, along with a mission statement and reason for pursuing the project.

- A list of objectives for the project.

- A collaborator/mentor who has been screened and has agreed to work with the group/individual.

- A list of at least three Common Core or state standards that will be mastered because of the project.

- A deadline for completion.

- The approximate point value for the project.

Short-term or progress deadlines help the students stay on task. If the group chooses a project that will take several weeks, short-term deadlines are crucial. In my class, students must earn 90-100 points per semester to earn an A, 80-89 points for a B, etc. If a team writes a proposal for an 80-point project that will require most of the semester, they are taking a huge risk. Long-term projects leave little room to fail if things don't work out. For example, if a project is estimated to take five weeks, and the mentor doesn't respond back for ten days, those days are lost, because students are required to collaborate. Sometimes groups will scramble for another mentor, adjusting as they go, while others just sit and wait… which is a bad idea.

Starter projects help offset risk and get students in the flow. These projects are worth 10-30 points and have a quick turnaround time. The idea is to fail early and often. Understanding the process and learning to foresee problems allow students to keep pushing forward or trash the project and move on, instead of wasting valuable time waiting for things to happen. This is not to say I don't accept failure… I do! In fact, embracing failure is important. But there's a powerful difference in learning from a completed project that didn't work out versus failing because they chose instead to wait around for something to happen.

STUDENTS MUST BLOG OR VLOG WEEKLY ABOUT THEIR RESULTS.

Every week, each group or individual must post a blog or vlog (video blog, if they prefer to deliver their message via YouTube). This practice serves three purposes:

1. It is a gradable task that helps maintain focus.
2. It gains valuable feedback from potential future mentors.
3. It allows them to grow the group's digital brand and is a platform on which to be seen as future leaders.

I found blogging and vlogging to be essential in the development of the Innovation Class projects. Reader comments really push students forward. Also, using social media, especially Twitter, to drive traffic to the blog/vlog is extremely helpful in getting feedback and gaining knowledge. In the past, some of my students have forged good relationships with Twitter All-Stars who re-tweeted their posts to 100,000 followers or more. That massive exposure really inspires students to keep going, and it's a good type of pressure. Students might not care if they disappoint the teacher with lackluster work, but I have found that they do not want to disappoint their network.

STUDENTS PRESENT THEIR PROJECT, TURN IN A REFLECTION, AND NEGOTIATE FOR THEIR GRADE.

When the project is finished, students must present their work to the key stakeholders. Sometimes stakeholders include the school board, other times it's me and/or their classmates. Occasionally, presentations are made off-campus at a collaborating business. Students prepare PowerPoint or Keynote presentations, along with some sort of deliverable: printed work, a prototype, etc. This requirement usually fulfills the presentation/oral skills standards quite nicely.

Upon completing the presentation, each student or group turns in a reflection. Here, the student explains what he or she took from the project and what standards were mastered in the process. Then, students negotiate for the point total because the students, consistently and predictably, ask for a higher point total than what the project is really worth.

This dance of negotiation is something I love. Often students will argue, sometimes passionately, and list reasons to defend their requests for a higher point total. Other groups gratefully take my first offer. I am more excited in assigning grades for these projects than I ever was in

> *Grades for my Innovation Class are **not simply a rubric**. Rather, students have an opportunity to **explain what they learned** from the project.*

my previous sixteen years of teaching. With the work and commitment most students put into their projects, they are able to substantiate their knowledge. Grades for my Innovation Class are not simply a rubric or a list of items. Rather, the reflection and negotiation offer students an opportunity to explain what they learned from the project. Some students are so passionate about what they have accomplished that they happily negotiate for a higher grade. If they are able to argue the point total in a clear and concise way (which, I believe, is a truly authentic assessment), I am happy to raise the grade.

A "Normal" Weekly Routine

Over the past year, I have talked to several teachers who are giving 20% Time a trial run. Some teachers are making it literally twenty percent of the school week and dedicating one entire class period. A slight majority of teachers choose Fridays. Ultimately, you won't know what works best for you and your students until you test the waters. Below, you'll see how

> Keep an
> **Innovation**
> **Idea Journal**
> handy.
> You never
> know when
> **inspiration**
> will hit.

time is allotted in my Innovation Class. If you want to try a 20% Time model in your class, you can simply change the daily task to a weekly or monthly task.

Monday: Brainstorming sessions, especially at the beginning of the semester. Toward the middle of the year, students feel equipped to take the initiative. Bring in items of inspiration: magazine articles, podcasts, blogs, and lots of TED talks!

Tuesday through Thursday: Individual research or collaboration with the experts, usually on Skype or Google Hangouts. Watch out for bad habits that can creep up during this time. For example, if the mentor isn't available, the group may be tempted to do other stuff, rather than accomplish the project goals.

Friday: Blog/vlog and give feedback to other teams. In addition to posting about their progress, Fridays are a day to talk about the ideas students have gathered throughout the week. These ideas may come from their own projects and even from their classmates' projects.

Like everybody else, students frequently get great ideas at odd times, like in the shower or while exercising. I suggest that students keep an Innovation Idea Journal or use their voice recorder function on their cell phone to save those thoughts to share later. You never know when inspiration will hit. Having a handy way to record ideas is vital!

What Does a Great Project Look Like?

Projects can take any number of forms and yield a variety of outcomes. The two following examples demonstrate how to handle failure successfully and how accomplishable projects don't have to take a long time. You'll read other examples of projects in Chapter 9.

ENVIRONMENTALLY FRIENDLY GROUNDS MAINTENANCE

One week, my class compiled a list of Things That Need Improvement on one side of a white board and wrote the solutions on the other. Stanford professor Tina Seelig calls the activity collecting-and-connecting in her book, *inGenius*. During the Monday brainstorming session, my student Mason put Grass Alternatives on one side of the board, and a big question mark on the solution side.

The school had several acres of grass that required maintenance during the year, and Mason assumed the cost was high. He didn't necessarily have a problem with the fact that the school had so much green space, but he knew the school's budget was very tight. He also questioned the use of the land. Obviously, the soccer and baseball fields needed the grass, but what about the vast sea of green in front of the school? Could it be better utilized?

A mass brainstorming session broke out. Could the school work with a farmer to grow vegetables and maybe use those vegetables in the school cafeteria? What about rock gardens? What about goats grazing on the school lawn? Like any good brainstorming session, no idea was shot down, but we realized that having corn growing in front of the school or goats grazing by the football field wouldn't enhance school morale. Mason re-defined his question: How could the school *more effectively* maintain the grass? A project was born! Mason and his project partner wrote up a proposal for finding cost-efficient solutions that would help the school save money and reduce its carbon footprint. They found two maintenance experts and a school employee to serve as mentors for the project, and they were off and running!

First they looked into alternative fuel lawn mowers. To their surprise, they learned some mowers on the market run on cooking oil. Their minds raced when they started to connect ideas together with this new information. Local restaurants normally had to pay to have the cooking oil and grease recycled. They would surely give the school the oil for free, right? Suddenly, they saw a new world of possibilities, including *free* fuel to power the mowers with an environmentally friendly solution!

With these new ideas coming to light, two school board members took an interest in the project because the lease on the older mowers was going to expire that summer. The project's visibility reached a new level when they were asked to present their findings at a special school board meeting. They pressed on, researched more, and talked to some local restaurants as well as the superintendent of school grounds. They even started to blog about the project. Several people—lawn equipment sales representatives as well as a few people who genuinely wanted to provide more insight—commented on the blogs. One reader replied back from South Korea! Unfortunately, most of the feedback warned of little cost efficiency and the trouble with getting the free oil.

After further investigation, the knowledge gained from their audience proved correct. The mowers carried a high price tag, and getting the free oil from restaurants meant buying equipment to collect and transport it back to school. If the driving motive was to save the school money, alternative fuel mowers weren't the answer. Project over.

Did the project produce an alternative to lawn costs and maintenance? No. Would I call this project a failure? Absolutely not! The students formed a great driving question, collaborated with experts and local stakeholders, and most importantly, took control of their learning opportunities... and knocked out some Common Core standards in the process. They still fulfilled the presentation obligation and presented their findings to the school grounds committee.

The class also learned that making decisions for an entire school involves mountains of red tape. Going forward, we stayed away from projects that involved the school and money. It is one thing to have a great idea, but it can be frustrating to implement those ideas in a world that requires school board approval and state budget committee reviews. The project helped us determine that, if we wanted to do school-related matters, we would work on smaller, more manageable projects... like the next example.

SPECIAL NEEDS CLASS COFFEE SHOP

In the same spirit of collecting-and-connecting, some students observed that the special needs students might want a more active role in the school. A few students felt that the class was too isolated and the student body didn't have the chance to connect with them. Another student mentioned that he would love it if he could buy a cup of coffee in the morning. Eyes lit up immediately... A coffee shop operated by the special needs class!

Peyton and Natalie took on the project immediately. They wrote a proposal, identified the core standards that would be mastered, found a mentor in a local coffee shop owner, and asked for permission to move forward with the special education teacher. Everyone involved felt happy with the win-win scenario. The coffee shop stood to get some great public relations out of the deal. The teacher was excited to work on a fun, meaningful project, and the students would get coffee in the morning!

Within two weeks, Peyton and Natalie had completed the project! The girls, like true entrepreneurs, started the business, made sure it was in good hands, and then moved on to the next project!

Both of these examples exemplify the value of real-world collaboration opportunities for students and show how student-led initiatives can create a better culture for schools. Although the environmental lawn project didn't work out the way the students had expected and the coffee shop project progressed more quickly than anticipated, both projects successfully created great learning opportunities and formed meaningful partnerships.

As a frame of reference, the environmental lawn project took five weeks, hit seven standards, and earned sixty points. The student-run coffee shop took two weeks, hit five standards, and earned thirty points. There is usually a week-to-point ratio, along with identifying more than three standards. That said, I prefer a well-constructed project

Student-led initiatives *can create a* **better culture** *for schools.*

rather than a reflection that was stretching the truth on a huge list of standards.

Regrets... I've Had a Few

Going back to the *Johnny Bunko* idea that there is no plan, I will say that a routine week might be rare, thus, the weekly schedule can and will change. Some groups valued the Monday brainstorming session, while other groups felt that they had to research or prototype during those days. I will also admit that I strayed from this structure in the second year of our Innovation Class, and that was a mistake. Things got lax, and I had a hard time refocusing students' attention on their deadlines. Another mistake I made was allowing students to start the semester with a big project. While it's nice to start off with a huge I'm-going-to-change-the-world type project, the class and grades are better if the students learn the system before diving into something large-scale. Knocking out smaller projects also gets them into a rhythm of project management.

I also have been too involved in finding the students' potential mentors. There was a time when I would spend hours scanning the web for people to help, rather than focusing on helping students with their day-to-day tasks. In reality, this was no different than a teacher grading papers while the students worked. While I was trying to help, my actions made some students too dependent on me; they relaxed knowing I would find a mentor for them. I have learned that it is better for students to find their own mentors than for me to recruit them. In the past

> *There is nothing wrong with **leading** students through a **brainstorming** session, but stop short of giving them the focus for a project.*

three years, we've been honored to be approached by some great leaders who offer their insights or talents to our class. When this happens, my standard response is to graciously ask them to be on standby and see if a student needs their expertise. Forcing a cool mentor on my students creates dependency, and might sway their choice on projects, ultimately reducing student freedom and voice.

Perhaps my worst mistake has been giving students a great project idea before they formed their own vision. There is nothing wrong with leading them through a brainstorming session, but stop short of giving them the focus for a project. Giving away a great idea usually causes jealousy because the other student groups see my involvement, however small, as an unfair advantage, especially if the project turned out to be successful. Student competition and jealousy can destroy the class, so be careful not to give away an idea for a great project. Instead, help enhance their ideas through feedback and class brainstorming.

Before you move on to the next chapter, think about how you could bring innovation to your classes or school.

- How could you introduce a class like this into your school? What would it take to get your school to allow such a course?

- How could your current personal learning network help your students?

- Could you offer this type of experience as a club?

- If you are a homeschool parent/instructor, how could you empower your network to form an Innovation Co-operative?

- If you are a parent, could you host your own Innovation Project and help find potential collaborators?

Don't wait for your administration to suggest an Innovation Class. Get creative! Start working within your existing courses to provide opportunities that allow students to take ownership of their education.

quick thoughts

- This is a project-based, passion-based course, so let the students feel free to choose to research a topic of their personal interest.
- Authentic collaborators bring a certain legitimacy to the learning process.
- To keep things streamlined, each student must submit a proposal with the standards, a timeline, and an approximate, fair point value.
- Students should blog about their results to keep the project running smoothly.
- A final presentation to key stakeholders is a great way to tie in the academic rigor to the real world aspect of project completion.

notes

4

Six Building Blocks of Innovative Learning

"Bueller? Bueller?"

Innovative education is a lot like the film, *Ferris Bueller's Day Off.* If you don't quite get what that means, don't worry. I didn't either at first. My wife, Alicia, made the connection one day as I shared updates on my Broadcasting and Innovation Classes. Amazed by the work my students had done and impressed by the partnerships they had formed, she made the *Ferris Bueller* comment. As much as I love great pop culture analogies, I had to ask her to elaborate.

The film's writer and director, John Hughes, paints a picture of the typical classroom, which features Ben Stein teaching American History. The all-too-familiar scene depicts the teacher talking in a monotone voice and the entire time without any interaction from the students. It was very funny to see a... Anyone? Anyone...? *stereotype* that hits very close to what American students experience in a traditional classroom.

Believing that school is an exercise in boredom, Ferris decides to skip school and create a memorable day. Because he does not want to spend it alone, he collaborates with his best friend, Cameron, and soon decides to include his girlfriend, Sloane, in the adventure. I'm assuming you've seen the movie, so I'll get to the point: *Ferris Bueller's Day Off* can be viewed as an allegory of a person escaping the traditional educational prison to learn on his own. He breaks rules (attendance), fails (when he places a phone call imitating Sloane's dad), innovates (dresses as Sloane's dad), takes huge risks (sings in a parade and poses as the Sausage King of Chicago), and ultimately experiences and learns more by traveling and traversing real-life situations. In short, he receives a much better education that day on his own than if he had gone to… Anyone…? Anyone…? *class.*

Our challenge is to take the positive lessons from *Ferris Bueller's Day Off* and apply them to an Innovation Class model. In this chapter, I'll offer examples and insights from great teachers from all over the world. You'll learn what they are accomplishing and how you can construct this sort of real-life, hands-on learning experience in the classroom.

Through trial and error and by talking with other educators who are implementing Innovation Classes or 20% Time in their schools, I've identified six components to innovative learning. These six building blocks are necessary whether you're devoting an entire class or a portion of a class period daily or weekly to student-defined, passion-based projects. Every such class needs to be: Collaborative, Task-Oriented, Daring, Relevant, Reflective, and Ongoing.

COLLABORATIVE: LOOK FARTHER THAN THE PERSON BESIDE YOU.

When I thought about the word *collaboration* five years ago, ice-breaking games, team-building exercises, trust falls, and other creative challenges came to mind. Having students pair up and discuss a predetermined prompt or experiment encouraged an obvious form of collaboration. I've since learned that collaboration should include networking with real-world experts, as well as other students.

When my students began collaborating with outside experts, I realized I no longer had to be the only teacher. My students quickly figured out that the classroom instructor doesn't have all the answers, and, in fact, is learning right along with them. It is powerful for students to work with one another, but I steer away from the textbook activities that instruct them to pair up to find a predetermined solution. Rather than relying on exercises for which the teacher provides the project and eventually the answers, I prefer for students to collaborate on open-ended projects where neither the students, nor I, know the answer. Allowing students to discuss issues and solve problems,

When my students began **collaborating** *with outside experts, I realized I no longer had to be* **the only teacher.**

with input from wise leaders as well as one another, empowers them to learn more and ask better questions.

Task-Oriented: Move from *What if...?* to a To-Do List.

One of the dangers of an Innovation Class is that students can get lost in ideals or theoretical scenarios. A project can stall out when the learner has a "big idea" but no real road map or understanding of how it will be executed. Being task-oriented helps move students from idea to *action*.

The top complaint I hear from teachers about their Genius Hour or 20% Time is that it starts off with excitement and then runs out of gas. Energy fills in the air when the students first ponder the possibilities in a new project. The brainstorming, enthusiasm, and feeling that they can change the world is exhilarating.

Then... *thud.*

What happens after the Big Idea? Too often nothing happens or, at least, not enough.

Feedback I have received from other teachers, as well as from observation in my own classes, indicates that the letdown is frequently due to a lack of task-oriented assignments. As I wrote in the previous chapter, designing a proposal with a set deadline is vital. But a deadline for the finishing date is not good enough. Great projects have several daily and weekly task deadlines. Tasks may include observations, experiments, interviews, data analysis, prototyping, or even reflections.

To keep students on target and excited about their progress, the teacher must show them how to build a calendar of events with several to-do lists along the way. It is acceptable and important to build in time for *What if…?* scenarios during the brainstorming sessions, but setting deadlines for deliverables is also essential.

DARING: BE BRAVE ENOUGH TO RISK FAILURE.

To many students, getting an A seems more important than actually learning the lesson. I can empathize with them. In college, I would spend several hours cramming for tests and end up scoring well, only to immediately forget much of the material. Fear of failure made me study hard, but the quest for the grade diminished the actual learning process. Although many students want to do meaningful work and be challenged beyond the classroom, the fear of what might happen to their grade stops them from trying daring projects.

Joseph Campbell, who was an expert on world mythology and religion, is often quoted for this bit of wisdom: "In the cave you fear to enter lies the treasure you seek." As I mentioned earlier, creating a culture that accepts and even encourages failure as part of the learning process helps diminish this fear. When students know they can trust that the teacher will not punish them for trial-and-error learning, they really start to push the limits of meaningful projects. My friend and fellow teacher Joli Barker, an elementary school teacher from Texas, calls this a *fearless classroom*.

> *Failure is a natural part of **daring to learn** by trial and error.*

48

Joli's students take risks by *gamifying* the learning experience. They are then willing to press reset (so to speak) on a game that needs to start over. Her goal is to help her fourth-grade students to adopt the attitude of fearlessness in their approach to learning. To that end, she inspires them to go beyond the easy stuff and stretch their comfort zones.

It is important to tell students that their projects will involve risks. They should be aware that they might fail to achieve the results they want. But please reassure them that failure for a project doesn't necessarily equate to receiving an F. Failure is a natural part of daring to learn by trial and error. After all, if a lesson is learned perfectly the first time, was it really worth learning?

By reassuring students that failure is expected and helpful, educators can empower them to go beyond wanting to do what the teacher requires and propel them to creative, active engagement! This is where most schools need to re-examine the purpose of the class. Is education about earning a grade, or is it really about fostering learning and creative engagement? We need to put the focus on the process of creativity and development, not on earning a grade for compliance.

RELEVANT: THE STUDENT BRINGS MEANING TO THE LESSON.

You've heard the question countless times: "When am I ever going to use this in real life?" Students want to work on projects that actually mean something. Some would even like to change the world. But when do they have time? Where do they find the discipline? Offering the opportunity to work on relevant projects is yet another way to spark students' engagement as well as increase their retention of knowledge.

Each semester I use the complaint, "When am I ever going to use this in real life?" as a challenge for my students to create something meaningful. I might say something like, "You don't like how school fails to relate to the real world? You don't see the connection between your math (or science, or history, or language arts) class and your future? Do something about it! Create a project that brings meaning to you. Make it relevant

> *Use the complaint, "When am I ever going to use this in real life?" as a **challenge** for students to **create something meaningful.***

and change lives!"

The challenge takes a previously held negative opinion about school and flips it. My students discover early on that they are responsible for their learning experiences and for bringing meaning to the class. It's in this environment that a student can have the epiphany: I *can change the world, bring value to my life, possibly help others,* and *earn a grade!* You will see joy on your students' faces when it dawns on them that they are in control of both their learning experiences and their purpose.

REFLECTIVE: LOOK BACK TO LEARN MORE.

After completing a project, or even a week's work, reflecting provides an opportunity to correct mistakes and identify necessary improvements for the next task. It's a powerful process that adds to the learning experience.

Reflections are usually accomplished by writing journals, blogging, vlogging, or formal essays. As with the brainstorming sessions that help students find their ideas, the class discussions about what the groups have learned provide additional value; each student offers unique insight.

I believe reflection is an equally important practice for teachers. I continue to adapt and hone the assignment requirements and expectations for my class, based on what I learn each year through student feedback and from my own observations. This is why no two Innovation Class projects are ever the same. On my fall semester and year-end finals last year, I had the students complete a reflection about how the class experience could be improved. Obviously, their projects comprised the bulk of the grade, but I wanted a reflection for two reasons. First, I wanted them to look back and see what they had accomplished, or, in some cases, how they came up short. Second, I wanted to improve as a teacher. I asked them to be brutally honest and assured them that their honesty would not affect their grade. Their insights and suggestions help me shape this ever-changing class.

Ongoing: The final bell isn't the end.

Whether a project lasts two weeks or the entire semester, *all* learning is ongoing. We should all be lifelong learners, always growing, always adapting. The real quest for teachers is to get students to understand and appreciate the value and joy of learning. I *love* my job as a teacher, especially teaching innovation and creativity, because each new day brings a new lesson. I embrace those opportunities! I love knowing that I will never run out of chances to learn from experts, life situations, different cultures, and my students. My desire is to instill in my students the same excitement and enjoyment I feel for learning.

But there's another side to the ongoing aspect of learning. Some projects can't be wrapped up in a few weeks' time or even by the end of the school year. I've discovered that students have different reactions when they realize their projects might not be complete when the final bell rings. For example, one project last year involved creating a 5k/10k run to raise funds for a childhood illness. After a decent turnout, several runners and families asked if the event could be repeated annually. The two students who created the project realized it would be ongoing and were excited to discover that they had created a legacy project. For other students, however, the possibility of an unfinished project causes them to shut it down prematurely. While I understand why a student wouldn't even want to start a project they couldn't finish by the end of the school term, I highly encourage them to push forward so they can follow a passion.

As the teacher, you can ease students' fears about grades by structuring a point system that takes into account accomplishable tasks and reflections along the way. The actual completion of the big project is not the point. What's most important are the learning and collaborative oppor-

> *We should all be **lifelong learners**, always growing, always adapting.*

tunities that go along with such projects.

Innovative Learning in Action

Taking these six traits into account, I wanted to offer examples of what an Innovation Class (or Genius Hour or 20% Time) looks like in different grade levels.

Andi McNair, a teacher at Bosqueville Elementary in Texas, decided to implement innovative learning in her classroom. While teaching a gifted/talented class, she began to consider ways that collaboration outside the building would benefit her students. McNair considered what Innovation Time might look like at the elementary level. After a few Skype calls to me and discussions with other Genius Hour teachers, McNair laid out the framework for her experiment.

Next, she brainstormed project ideas with her students. Some of the ideas were wacky, some serious, and some impossible, but what all the ideas shared in common was passion! The students were fired up about getting to learn about things they were interested in. She asked if I would Skype her class and listen to the project proposals. Upon hearing ideas, like working with animals or designing a video game, I asked them if they ever thought about learning from someone other than Ms. McNair. The idea shocked them. Some looked nervously at her, and a couple even said, "*She* is our teacher." But when she asked if they would like to learn about animals from a person who worked at a shelter, their eyes lit up! They immediately understood the value of collaboration in that moment: Ms. McNair is the teacher, and we can still learn from other experts *with* her.

I still Skype her classroom to check up on the student projects and what they've learned. I've also had the pleasure of hearing from her about how the experiment improved her teaching experience. I asked her to reflect on her first year of implementing an innovation time. She wrote:

Since introducing an Innovation Time in my classroom, my role as teacher has completely changed. I learned about Innovation by connecting with you and other teachers on Twitter. I no longer stand at the front of the room and teach but instead allow my students to connect, collaborate, and engage in activities that encourage problem solving and critical thinking.

This time gives my students the opportunity to address real world problems. Their passion is at the center of their project, and this makes the learning meaningful for them. Our students learn best when they make connections and the learning is driven by their passions.

Initially, I wasn't sure how the Innovation model would succeed in an elementary classroom. I was concerned that students would struggle with project design and creation. However, when given the freedom to design their own projects based on their passions, my students came up with several inspiring ideas.

Some of the projects my students worked on were:

- Introducing Augmented Reality to Teachers.

- Planning a 5K Run to Raise Money for Cancer.

- Finding Ways to Decrease Animal Euthanasia.

- Creating and Sharing New Ice Cream Flavors.

- Sharing Why Snakes are not All Bad.

- Teaching Others How to be Safe While Hunting.

- Finding Ways to Make Local Hospitals More Comfortable.

- Creating a Website for Students to Share Book Reviews.

While I know that some of the projects will not work out and students will struggle along the way, I also realize that this is what makes Innovation unique and perfect for my classroom.

I want my students to learn how to fail, how to struggle, and most importantly how to try again. As their teacher, I should be preparing them for the real world, rather than a place where every problem has a correct answer and all of their questions can be answered by an adult or a textbook.

My students have enjoyed Innovation Time and look forward to class each week. They often come into my room during lunch and other free times to work on their projects. Because they are passionate about their topics, they have a desire to work on their projects. They have ownership in the learning and, because of this, they are inspired to do more, create more, and search for answers. They are intrinsically motivated by their curiosity about the topics that they have chosen.

Integrating Innovation into the Curriculum

Joy Kirr, a middle school teacher in Elk Grove, Illinois, has incorporated a Genius Hour into her 80-minute English class. For her students, the spark of ideas comes from the assigned reading. Students are then challenged with specific tasks to enhance the material. She uses popular fiction titles to awaken their imaginations, and then implements the skills of non-fiction writers, such as Angela Meiers, to find teachable moments.

Kirr got the idea for her course—Read. Be Inspired. Act on it.—from another educator, Erin Olson (@eolsonteacher). She ran with it, and her execution of the process is impressive. What I really love is that Kirr's students get to collaborate with one another, as well as outside experts, to create various projects. Specific tasks separate each step: a brainstorming session, task assignments and completion, and the final product.

To Kirr, and other teachers who embrace this sort of learning, crafting the students' voices is important, and their voices must be present in more than class discussion. That's where their blogs and vlogs come into play. While it's fun and helpful to discuss ideas in class, creating online evidence of education strengthens the students' learning experiences. Additionally, their work provides a road map for educators who may be looking for ideas on how to execute an Innovation Class, Genius Hour, or 20% Time. You'll read more about the value of social media and other digital tools later in this book, but I want to point out here that these middle school students are serving as the teachers to others through their blogs and vlogs.

Creating online evidence of education strengthens the students' learning experiences.

The way Kirr integrates a Genius Hour time into her normal curriculum is masterful. The class watches educational YouTube videos, creates goal sheets, and engages in awesome class discussions. They work to solve real-world issues. Interestingly, the course idea was ignited by fiction books that are a part of her regular independent reading curriculum. She has woven a blend of passion and collaboration with fiction and fact.

Innovation through Game Design and Design Thinking

At Pimpama State Secondary School in Australia, Rhys Cassidy and Dave Harman use Design Thinking to harness creativity and innovation. I met teacher Rhys Cassidy on Twitter. He and fellow teacher Dave Harman, an experienced software-developer-turned-teacher, have been teaching *Playmakers* to two middle-school level classes. *Playmakers* seeks to combine design and systems thinking by leveraging students' interests in games to enable learners to seek out and creatively solve problems.

The course began with an introduction to games design and systems thinking using Gamestar Mechanic, an online game design community. Students were challenged to produce a game that emulated any system in the universe (e.g. biological, political, quantum) and developed players' empathy in order to encourage them to change the system for the better. Among a range of games, from simple platform games that mirrored small business, to more complicated top-down games designed to re-create climate change, one female student's game stood out. She had enrolled late in the course, having transferred from another subject that she found difficult due in part to her perceptual differences attributable to her diagnosis of Autism Spectral Disorder (ASD). The student's game was a top-down, simple role-playing game that emulated a system of child labor. She used message blocks to incorporate a narrative that exhibited wry humor and a heck of a lot of empathy and left players with a desire to eradicate child labor. These were impressive outcomes from a student who could find it difficult to communicate, empathize, or engender empathy in others.

The next unit required students to once again mirror a system but, this time, one that directly and currently impacted the school. Systems chosen included the canteen line, public transport, and cyber-bullying. Each group of four students interviewed the school's principal to gather data about their chosen system. Then, based on feedback and reflections, each group designed games using specific software. At the beginning of each lesson, the class had a five-minute presentation during which the groups were asked, "What are your impediments?," "What is going well?," and "What needs improving?" This process, along with a system of rotating roles, was designed to make each student accountable, foster transparency, and drive constant improvement.

Innovative learning is Collaborative, Task-Oriented, Daring, Relevant, Reflective, and Ongoing.

Lastly, Rhys asked students to reflect on their learning via a blog that could be shared for a digital audience. The blog alternative worked especially well for those students who found it difficult to share in front of the class during the five-minute, stand-up presentation. The reflection was also a nice way for the students to wrap up the project and served as an ongoing reminder of the rewards that challenging projects can provide for students and their schools.

In all three of these examples of innovative learning in action, the classes demonstrated what it means to be collaborative. The classes function well because they are very task-oriented and have specific deadlines, manageable responsibilities, and assignments along the way. The projects were daring. In addition to the ever-present fear of failure, these projects pushed well beyond the bounds of normal day-to-day class. The projects were relevant, mostly because the students had a choice in designing the activities and learning about topics they found meaningful. And each class used reflective practices, such as journaling and participating in mentor-led discussions. Lastly, the ongoing nature of the class is exhibited because each project's lessons enhanced the next project, a future class, or, in some cases, extended beyond the classroom.

Now that you've seen a few examples of what innovation can look like in the classroom, I want to show you how social media can be harnessed to enhance the learning experience. In the next chapter, we'll examine what social media is and acknowledge what it isn't.

quick thoughts

- Collaboration means more than working with fellow students.

- Teachers can encourage daring, meaningful projects.

- Creating a culture that allows risk and embraces failure is vital in learning.

- Students want to know that what they are working on matters for reasons other than "Because it's on the test." The more relevant projects you can bring to students, the better.

- It's important to encourage student action beyond the classroom. When students understand that the classroom can be a testing ground for something of long-term value, their concept of education transforms.

notes

5

Social Media & Teachers

The two words *Twitter* and *teachers* don't typically go together, especially with adults over age thirty. In fact, many educators seem to have a mental block about Twitter. Some see social media as a waste of time or place to brag. And since, generally speaking, teachers aren't boastful (modest is a better descriptor), they just don't appreciate the value of Twitter and other social media platforms. If you can relate, this chapter is for you.

When it comes to finding great ideas and attracting pro-level collaborators—which we will get to in Chapter 7—for both you and your students, social media is *the* game changer. That's why I'm convinced that teachers need to embrace social media and that our students need to be connected as well.

Twitter and YouTube have been the absolute best tools in my teaching career, and I have used Twitter for only the past two years. In that time, these two sites have become my primary resource for professional development. While I do find value in (some of) the in-service days at my school, YouTube and Twitter are my daily go-to sources for inspiration and professional development. As valuable as these resources are for me, they are incredibly useful for student growth as well.

To help you understand why I feel so strongly about Twitter, I have to go back to July 2012. I was presenting at Microsoft's Partners in Learning Educator Forum, where I met educational leader Alan November. He had reviewed my students' work, and wondered why he had never come across my name or heard about my class. The conversation went something like this:

"This is awesome, Don, but I can't believe I haven't seen your students' work before."

"Well, I'm from Indianapolis and you're from Boston, so I guess that's why," I replied.

"Yeah, but I'm surprised I haven't seen any of this come across Twitter."

"I don't have a Twitter."

"Huh? Why not?"

"Because Twitter is for self-righteous celebrities. I'm not to be mistaken for a Kardashian."

"Twitter is for teachers, Don. They are one of the biggest groups on there. You really need to sign up, so more teachers can see your students' work."

"I don't want to brag. It will come across as boastful," I replied.

"It's not bragging; it's sharing best-practices. Wouldn't you like to borrow some ideas off of a teacher that was doing cool stuff in a class like yours?"

A light bulb came on in my head. I got it. I started my Twitter account on the spot. Actually, Alan demanded I go to the site right then and there to set up my account.

Finding a Supportive Community

Ever since that fateful day in July, I have become a better teacher and a more responsible role model. I mentioned earlier that I taught broadcasting for five years. Before that, I taught middle-school English for ten years. While I had received some video training back in my college days, when I took over the broadcasting class, the equipment was foreign to me. Empowering my students to learn *with* me proved to be an effective method for getting off the ground. In recent years, I have discovered that every tutorial is on YouTube. If something breaks, watch a fix on YouTube. Need a new software update? Learn the steps on YouTube. Your camera's codec isn't compatible with the software…? You get my point.

*When it comes to **finding great ideas** and **attracting pro-level collaborators**, social media is the game changer.*

YouTube also expanded my vision for student-produced videos. As other high schools posted student videos, the possibilities in my mind for my students opened up. I thought we were doing a good job; then I saw videos from Ladue and Hillcrest, both located in Missouri. These programs put most colleges to shame. The video quality, the script writing, and the professionalism far exceeded my expectations for a high school media class.

Shortly after I got on Twitter, I shared some of my students' videos on YouTube and tweeted out a link. A week later, I started using appropriate hashtags like #PowerofVideo and #StuVideo. An hour after posting with those hashtags, I received a message from our school's media specialist who suggested I follow Don Goble. After a quick search, I discovered that Goble taught at Ladue High School. Remembering the other school with an amazing program, I searched on Twitter for HTV Magazine and Hillcrest High School. I found that Hillcrest had its own Twitter account, as does the instructor, Dave Davis.

I immediately reached out to Don and Dave, and both agreed to share insights into running a successful broadcasting program. After picking Don's brain for techniques and tips, he asked me if I wanted any of his notes, lesson plans, or the syllabus to his class. I was shocked that he wanted to share everything. I am a very competitive person, and the reason our class watched so many videos from Don's and Dave's schools was because we were driven to be as good, and in time, better than they were. We watched these student-produced videos with a mix of awe and jealousy. Selflessly, Don was handing me the knowledge he had collected during the past fifteen years. I felt a little guilty accepting his generosity, but I did so graciously. Within the hour he'd sent me an email with over twenty attachments including lesson plans, tips, and tutorials. *Bam!* Just like that, I became a better teacher.

Don's kindness taught me about being open and wanting to make other teachers more effective through collaboration. This sharing culture is the *special sauce* of social media. I don't know if I would be as open and as sharing had I not met Don and Dave. Their example shifted my thinking. I transformed from a teacher who was trying to beat other schools' video departments, to one who understands that collaborating openly with other schools makes us all more successful. Iron sharpens iron.

Suddenly, we could collaborate, pair up our students, and share in the joy of creating videos for other schools. Before, our focus was more on watching the competition and loathing them for having better equipment (or whatever excuse we could come up with). If you ever want to see a prime example of two schools collaborating, go to *mustangmorningnews.com* and do a search for "Ladue." You'll see how Don Goble's Ladue program and Mira Costa High School have worked together to co-produced each other's school video packages. Mira Costa, in California, took a theme like academic cheating and produced it for Don's school in Missouri. The results are not only quality, they're cool. It's remarkable to see video production and collaboration from across the country!

Dave Davis of Hillcrest High School has also been instrumental in my students' development. While not as active on

> **Twitter** is not just for the Kardashians. It **serves as a tool** for **discovering** amazing teachers who are **sharing** what works for them.

Twitter, he uses the site to announce upcoming videos and drive traffic to the HTV website. After watching Hillcrest's videos, my students took the imitation-is-the-best-form-of-flattery mantra to a new level. We saw what worked for them and gave it a try. Hillcrest has done live streaming broadcasts, called Buzz-a-Thons, as a fundraiser for several years. The funds go toward a life-changing trip that HTV students get to take every summer or Spring Break. In previous years, they have traveled to Hawaii or taken long, amazing bus trips. After watching HTV, my students decided to host a similar telethon-type of event to see if they could achieve the same results. While we didn't earn as much money, the process and actual broadcast made for an incredible learning experience, and I have Dave Davis and his unbelievable crew at HTV to thank.

My story of finding mentors on Twitter is not uncommon. I have heard from countless teachers who credit social media (Twitter, most often) for the source of professional development and inspiration. Thus, Twitter is not just for the Kardashians. It serves as a tool for discovering amazing teachers who are sharing what works for them. In some cases, they're sharing what doesn't work for them, which is also valuable.

My main point about Twitter is that it allows us to celebrate and share best practices within the school and across the country. Much like when a principal asks a new teacher to collaborate with and learn from a master teacher down the hall, Twitter offers the potential for community and mentorship. However, there seems to be a lack of acceptance, or maybe skepticism, by some teachers when it comes to sharing their curriculum on Twitter.

Aw shucks....

Teachers are a modest bunch; they don't like to brag. Don't get me wrong: when test results come, a sense of pride permeates the school. Healthy competition exists between teachers within departments, especially when comparing passing rates and growth. However, this pride tends to be confined within each department. It's rare to hear a teacher announcing over the PA that he or she had the best results in the building;

that would feel like bragging. For many, posting best-practice insights on Twitter for the world to see is out of the question. However, just like my previous, falsely held opinion about Twitter being exclusively for look-at-me celebrities, many teachers miss the point: If you are an awesome teacher and have found something that works, you need to share that knowledge with the educational community. It isn't bragging; it's *helping*. Other teachers will not accuse you of showing off. In fact, I believe that social media, if used correctly, is the ultimate teachers' lounge. It's the perfect place to share best practices. So let's lose the "Aw shucks, it's just me" attitude and start sharing!

Opening the channels of communication is the key to successful, educational reform. It drives me crazy when a politician tells me what should work or when an educational expert (who has never taught before) tells me their theories about what they know is best! Teachers know that theories can never explain a child's lack of interest that's caused not by a boring curriculum but by worry about his parents' fighting. Standardized tests can't force a student to work at grade level when the fact that his family moves with every eviction notice keeps him distracted and behind the rest of the class. Teachers are the experts because we've learned to account for and respond to thousands of variables in the classrooms.

> *If you have found something that works, **share that knowledge** with the educational community. It isn't bragging; it's **helping**.*

Too often, when teachers find an innovative approach to teaching or make a correlation between a new method and improved student performance, they are hesitant to share it with others. They think, "Well that just worked for me and my classroom," or "I don't think that would work anywhere else," or worst yet, "I don't want to brag."

64

But if—and this was the big breakthrough for me—we are tired of taking advice from politicians and clinical experts who have never worked with the types of students in our classrooms, then we must find a way to share information with the real educational community. Social media has been a powerful resource for me. I'm confident that as more educators embrace it, its impact will multiply.

Which Platform is Best?

Teachers often ask me what social media outlet is best for education. It ultimately boils down to personal choice. Here are some insights that may help you find your preferred community, be it Twitter, Facebook, Pinterest, or Instagram.

TWITTER VERSUS FACEBOOK: QUANTITY VERSUS QUALITY

Twitter is a social media platform that allows you to *follow* people. The appeal to the site is that you can get an inside view to someone's insights, and they don't have to follow you back. That's why so many celebrities like Twitter: They can send out messages to their fans without having to follow back thousands, or millions, of fans. Messages are limited to 140 characters, so each tweet is a short, concise, twenty- to thirty-word message.

With Facebook—if you set your status updates to private, which I recommend—both individuals have to *friend* one another to see the updates. Post lengths aren't as limited, so messages can go into greater depth.

For me, Twitter has been a *quantity* site for educational discussion, whereas the *quality* of individual discussions can be higher on Facebook. For example, if I post a question on Twitter, I get several quick, thought-provoking answers that point me to additional research and solutions. Facebook group pages—topic-focused pages that allow people not following each other to communicate without friending everyone in the group—allow me to ask questions and receive in-depth answers. This is where Facebook has the edge on quality. Because users are not constrained to 140 characters, they can post more comprehensive comments and go into detail.

Honestly, I tend to use Facebook more for family events and sharing personal memories with friends. I post pictures of my children, vacations, and personal items more on this site because my parents live in another state. I preserve and revisit my family memories on this site by posting photographs from vacations and holidays. I might post an update about my favorite sports teams winning or losing or drop a line to a classmate I graduated with in high school. Because I've set my privacy settings to private, I have control over who sees what. That means I don't have worry about who sees the pictures of my five year old that I've posted on my personal page or who reads my reaction to the Colts losing in the playoffs.

As much as I like Facebook for personal use, I've found Facebook's group pages, which are much like clubs, to be excellent forums to exchange ideas and find solutions. The group participants can only read my posts on that specific page.

My favorite Facebook groups usually develop from conferences I attend during the summer. While at these conferences and/or workshops, I, or someone else as excited about social media as I am, start a Facebook group page. Because of the great relationships that are formed at events like these—think summer camps when you were a kid—we welcome a landing site to continue the discussion. To me, the Microsoft Partners in Learning U.S. Forum group is like a family. Seventy to eighty teachers attended the event, but the Facebook group only has about thirty active users. Since the conference, these users have posted questions and shared methods, successes, failures, and trial-and-error experiences. Most importantly, we support each other. Many of these teachers are risk-takers, and they share their frustrations and discoveries. Some call out for collaboration and seek other classes that want to be a part of a global project. People post job openings when they come across opportunities and even celebrate little victories in their daily classroom life. In short, this group has become that ultimate teachers' lounge and psychiatrist office all in one. I subscribe to other groups on Facebook that serve other purposes. General groups, like Multimedia Teachers or Transforming Education, are bigger in nature and less personal but, nonetheless, excellent for sharing knowledge.

Can you use Twitter in a similar way to create a community? The answer is yes and no. Hashtags (#), such as #EdTech, #edu, #FlippedClass, etc., can lead you to like-minded people. But a hashtag search isn't as convenient as visiting specific group pages on Facebook. Hashtags are Twitter's killer app. The hashtag is used as a marker to look up information within all Twitter messages. So, if I want to read posts about education, I can do a search for #education, #EdChat, #EdTechChat, or #InELearning. By using these hashtags, any Twitter user can access great discussions and posts, and they do not have to subscribe to a specific group.

> You can get a **greater quantity** of information via Twitter and **more in-depth information** via Facebook.

I also use Twitter's list feature to create and keep track of people I want to follow or with whom I want to dialogue. The biggest disadvantage to a list is that, while other users can subscribe to a list, it is usually just curated and used as a group by the person who set it up. Thus, the visibility of a group discussion is buried within a list, which may or may not be open for subscription.

In short, you can get a greater quantity of information via Twitter and more in-depth information via Facebook.

INSTAGRAM AND PINTEREST

Instagram is a social media tool that heavily relies on pictures to convey the message. You can add messages and hashtags to your images and, if you choose, link them to your Facebook and Twitter. Instagram's primary purpose, however, is to crafting messages through images. The saying,

"A picture is worth a thousand words," aptly applies to this social media platform. And since it is easily accessed through smartphones, Instagram is a handy tool for on-the-go sharing.

How can you use Instagram for education? Take pictures of classroom activities and on field trips. Create a student-of-the-week photo opportunity. Showcasing student work is probably the most popular with students and parents. Parents love to get on their phone and see a picture of their child's work! But there can be more to Instagram than spotlighting student work.

Dave Guymon, a middle school teacher in Idaho, recently published an article for *Edutopia* in which he demonstrated how Instagram played a role in a poetry unit. After his students read "The Road Not Taken," he asked them to take pictures of what they thought the poem stood for, which was more than just roads. Using a simple hashtag to locate these photos, the class and teacher could see, literally, how Frost's poem made an impact on each student's life. This creative project allowed students to process the meaning of the poem and scan the world for visual representations of the theme—real world applications for a poem!

Instagram's photo sharing capabilities can also be a call to action. I have come across several examples of teachers who've sent students out to document social service activities or reinforce a theme from the class into acts of service, like volunteering opportunities or simply helping a lady carry her groceries to her car. By taking and posting pictures of good deeds, students transfer what they've learned into action and have the potential to inspire other students and adults to join in as well!

Pinterest is another visual social media tool that many educators enjoy. Like the misconceptions I had about Twitter, I used to think Pinterest was for other people: people who wanted to share recipes, post pictures of great room decorations, and show off new fashions. While I admit I'm not as familiar with this site, I've met several teachers who really know how to utilize this picture-friendly tool.

Erin Klein, an elementary school teacher in Michigan, is a Pinterest expert. Her wildly popular blog, *Kleinspiration*, is a smorgasbord of tips, ideas, and inspiration to transform a regular classroom into an engaging one. For Klein, Pinterest has been a place to visually collaborate with her fellow second grade teachers. Each day, the teachers *pin* educational ideas, apps, and fresh lesson ideas so they can share their findings in a weekly planning period. She also has a public Pinterest board where other teachers can collaborate and pin ideas as well. The platform allows educators from all over the world to find and curate sites that visually demonstrate what great lessons, poster boards, and classrooms look like.

> By **posting pictures of good deeds**, students **transfer** what they've **learned into action** and have the potential to **inspire others** as well!

Klein's Pinterest collaboration doesn't end with fellow teachers. Parents, too, can pin to a class board, which is usually kept private for the sake of security. This allows parents who might otherwise be too busy to volunteer at school to chip in. Klein told me that these class boards are different each year and are always popping with new ideas. Whether it is a new math app, short story idea, or field trip suggestion, the collective ideas pinned on the class board connect the parents and teacher. Educators frequently talk about collaboration, but collaboration with the parents is rarely mentioned. Klein has found a way to make her class planning and educational experiences truly collaborative by involving the people who know her students best… their parents.

YOUTUBE: ULTIMATE POSSIBILITIES

YouTube has turned the video world upside down and is stealing market share from traditional television networks. No longer do you need expensive equipment, a staff of writers, or actors to produce great videos. YouTube is making overnight celebrities of vloggers, music video produc-

> *I would hate for a student to go through the laborious process of filming and editing a video **for only one person to see.***

ers, and cats. People love cats... but education? You might be surprised at just how many educational videos are on YouTube.

I am biased toward YouTube because I taught broadcasting. Video is my medium of choice, and this platform shows off what students can do. In fact, about seventy percent of my broadcasting students have their own YouTube channel. They like the extra exposure our schools' channel provides, but each wants to drive traffic to his/her own channel, which we do with Twitter and Facebook.

In my opinion, nothing trumps video for social media and online exposure. I love reading blogs, but I am convinced that video web logs (vlogs) get the job done better because of the visual aspect. You may be thinking, "Yeah, but you taught classes in video production. Why should YouTube be considered important to a math, science, or social studies teacher?" The answer is Khan Academy.

I am not going to focus on the quality of Khan Academy videos here, other than to say I think they are somewhat dry, but effective, nonetheless. What I love about Khan is that lessons are visual, and students can watch the videos on demand, over and over, until they get the lesson.

Another interesting use of YouTube for any subject is the Flipped Classroom model. The Flipped Classroom concept has gotten a lot of buzz lately. Although I am not an expert on this style of teaching, I will say that this group knows the power of multimedia. For those of you not savvy with Flipped Classroom, the model is this: Create a video, or audio podcast, of the traditional lecture for students to watch or listen to at home. When the students come to school the next day, they do what would have traditionally been homework practice. The school lecture is flipped to be homework; the homework practice now replaces lecture time in school.

YouTube is filled with thousands of tutorials on how to edit film, learn software, build *Minecraft* villages, solve equations, make crafts, etc. If there is a demand for a product or service, you can be sure that there is a YouTube tutorial for it. In the past year, I turned to YouTube to learn how to turn off that darn *check engine* light on my car dashboard, install a vinyl floor, and get ink stains out of leather. A quick YouTube search and *voilà*! Videos *show* me how to fix my problems and make learning easy.

But YouTube has yet another purpose. I believe one of the most valuable and under-used methods of using YouTube for education is demonstrating mastery.

Mastery, Thoreau, and Everything After

When I was a sophomore in high school, I received an A and got really upset with my high school English teacher. We had just covered Transcendentalism, and my teacher wanted the traditional essay-and-poster combo to wrap up the unit. If I really wanted to go out of my way, she suggested a diorama. I asked her if I could do a video instead of the poster. I would still write the essay, but I really wanted to use my neighbor's new VHS camera and this seemed like a good excuse. (This camera was a really big deal in 1989. It recorded on regular VHS tapes i*n color, with sound!*)

I planned out my shots—modern video editing tools were not available to the masses yet—did my run-throughs, and filmed my project. It was amazing, as I would like to remember. I did a *compare and contrast* on the theme of Emerson and Thoreau's vision of how we should live versus the reality of modern society. I even threw in some humor, a soundtrack, and a guest appearance by my dog in this masterpiece. In short, I learned more from this project than I would have done with a poster, even a diorama. I turned it in and got an A. That's it. No public screening, no congratulations, no Oscar. Just an A. I had never before felt so empty about receiving an A.

Today, YouTube and Twitter erase that void. I never intend to be the sole audience for a video assignment. In fact, I would hate for a student to go through the laborious process of filming and editing a video for only one person to see. YouTube and Twitter provide an *audience*, meaning not just the educational buzz phrase, but an authentic, engaged audience.

My students use Twitter as the first amplification tool to get people to visit their YouTube page. Yes, some students already have YouTube subscribers (more on that in the student social media section), but their Twitter posts are advertisements that draw the audience to the video. I use Twitter as an amplification tool for my students as well. On average, I have more Twitter followers than my students; when I tweet something, it has a greater reach. If you were to look over my Twitter messages, many of them are directing my audience toward student work. Having a good social media network allows you to learn from other educators, but it also allows you, the teacher, to become an agent for your students.

Because many of my Twitter followers are in education, they're often happy to click over and watch a student-produced, YouTube video. I routinely direct friends to a student blog or project; and because teachers know lots of people, the message quickly gets passed along. Pretty soon, our reach extends way beyond the school district and shines a spotlight on what students are doing in the classroom. How many stories have you heard about because it went *viral?* Social media, specifically YouTube, is the catalyst for getting our students' work noticed. The media wants positive stories about education! Yes, they will report about the negative aspects of education, but segments, like NBC's *Education Nation* and *Making a Difference,* prove that they also *want* to spotlight the great things that are going on in the classroom. It isn't up to the students alone to find that authentic audience. It's our responsibility as teachers to showcase great student work.

Now, when my students produce a video or work on a project for my class, they know that they are not just trying to impress me; they are producing it for the masses. Yes, I want the students to make the class project priority one. Knowing that the public will see their work incentivizes them to make their projects even better. By putting the video on public display, they may be criticized or applauded. They also may get better feedback from their audience than just one teacher's opinion. The best part is, you never know when a class project may go viral.

Social media, *specifically* YouTube, is the catalyst *for getting our* students' work *noticed.*

Last year, two of my students produced a ten-minute documentary on their wrestling coach, Bob Haseman. After spending time getting interviews, writing the script, filming, and editing, they turned in the film to me to be graded. This project served a dual purpose; it was also submitted for our film festival. They earned a good grade from me, but I didn't expect the 2,000 views it received on YouTube within the first forty-eight hours. As they later learned, Bob Haseman is a big deal in the wrestling circles for Indiana. When they used Twitter to announce the documentary and YouTube link, it was re-Tweeted by several people. Those people passed it on to others who passed it on... you get the picture.

When I did my compare/contrast film about Ralph Waldo Emerson and Henry David Thoreau, I had an audience of one, with the feedback, "Great job, Don!" written on my essay. When Casey and John finished their documentary, they received a grade and a bit of praise and feedback from me. But when the YouTube community took to it, they received the validity of having a video that was seen by thousands. They also learned to accept compliments and criticisms of their work.

A second example of the power of YouTube came out of our Innovation Class. Eight years ago, a grade school student was stabbed to death not far from our school. The police have not caught the killer to this day. Several attempts have been made to re-ignite people's interest and get leads on the case, but nothing has worked. Then Mason, a senior in the Innovation Class, asked if we could do a short Public Service Announcement (PSA) video reminding the locals about the case. He also knew that a student-produced PSA would get a fair amount of media attention. So

Mason worked with Austin, my talented broadcasting producer, to put together a ninety-second package. They posted it on YouTube, and the local movie theater started showing it before each movie.

Within weeks, two television stations and two newspapers came to the school to do interviews. As it turned out, Mason was correct; having students produce PSAs is a great story on its own and leads to more coverage for the PSA's focus. Three weeks later, the State Attorney General called to say that Mason and Austin would receive a service award at the next City Council meeting. With the cinema placement, television spots, and newspaper articles, the video created more awareness and helped raise additional money for the reward.

The experience was life-changing. While Austin and Mason admit that they have worked on much harder video projects, nothing else has felt more important. Their goal was to produce a video not just for a grade, but for the entire city. They are hopeful that the PSA will eventually lead to an arrest. The reality is that these two students might be able to help bring justice to a grieving family. And it all started out as an idea from a class. Words can't express how this makes me feel as a teacher and father.

quick thoughts

- Social Media is a powerful tool of collaboration. Sharing ideas is not bragging!

- Twitter is a quick, effective medium to demonstrate what works in your class and to borrow ideas that are working for other educators.

- Facebook is more open to conversation and provides a platform for in-depth discussion. Please be careful not to rant.

- Pinterest and Instagram are great platforms to craft messages that offer visual appeal. They also provide collaborative and artistic opportunities.

- YouTube is the game changer in showcasing student work. It offers unparalleled opportunities to learn from tutorials produced by teachers and students.

notes

6

SOCIAL MEDIA & STUDENTS

A note before we begin: This chapter is about social media and students. I have written from the vantage point of the middle school and high school level. I understand the Internet poses unique risks for younger children. For this reason, elementary schools may choose to have students work in an enclosed network that limits or eliminates communication with the general public while allowing them to learn valuable skills. (I have three children, all under the age of thirteen who, for their protection, are not allowed to use social media. However, my oldest will begin her journey of responsible social media practice this year.) As I'll explain in this chapter, I believe that purposeful social media training propels our students' success. Obviously, safeguards, expectations, and proper supervision need to be in place, regardless of the student's age.

It baffles me that many high schools completely block social media sites like Twitter, Facebook, Instagram and YouTube. Some schools tolerate these sites but do not encourage them. The most common reason I hear for schools blocking social media is that the administration doesn't trust the students or that a few students ruined it by posting threats, sexual comments, or hurtful rumors.

While I understand why many school administrators feel skittish about allowing social media on the school network, I disagree with that decision. First, social media sites can be valuable tools. Second, not allowing the sites on the school network won't discourage students from using them. Isn't a greater service to teach students how to use social media safely and appropriately? Think about how dangerous a car can be with a new driver behind the wheel. Few people suggest banning cars at school. Instead, we instruct students on how to safely operate a car. The same principle applies to social media.

Yes, social media has been used inappropriately in the past. My heart aches when I hear of a student who has taken his or her life because cyber-bullying became unbearable. I get frustrated when I hear about a girl making a bad decision to *sext* message her boyfriend, only to find out that the entire school has seen what she intended to be kept private. Even teachers occasionally misuse social media by posting negative comments about their job, co-workers, or worse, their students! And sure, many students mimic the behavior of their favorite celebrities on social media with annoying habits, like talking about themselves in a not-so-flattering manner. The OMGs, LOLs, and duck-faced selfies *do not* impress prospective employers or school administrators. With all that said, however, let me make my case for why I still *love* social media.

Shifting Social Media from Negative to Positive

The common perception of today's teen is not a pretty one. Search Google for Generation Y or Millennial and you'll find descriptors like *self-absorbed*, *Me Generation*, and *lazy*. A few positive traits such as *civic-minded* and *politically active* come across, but it seems many pundits believe our students lack direction, have little motivation, and want to hang out rather than get a job. Unless you are Kramer from *Seinfeld*, this type of behavior is annoying at best. Moreover, many teachers and parents I talk to actually blame social media for their students' lack of motivation. That doesn't have to be the case. You *can* teach your students how to rise above the average social media butterfly.

*Students can grasp the **importance** of **social media as a tool** that should be used and **respected**.*

Many employers use social media to look for dirt when they are considering hiring a job applicant. They are not only looking for the gossip, reports on the best weekend parties, or inappropriate selfies. They're also looking for the complaints: *work sucks, school sucks, classmates on a project suck*, etc. A chronic-complainer is *not* the type of person prospective employers want.

My Twitter network is public and thus open to current students. But I have a personal policy of not accepting Friend invites from students on Facebook until after they've graduated. I enjoy reading about their journey into The Real World as they head into college and pursue a career. But nothing is more disappointing than reading a constant stream of negative posts. Some complain about how much they hate their boss or the job itself. Others make blanket statements like, "I hate all of you; none of you are my friends." These posts often indicate a downward spiral toward depression and lack of progress into adulthood. Unfortunately, these former students don't understand why they cannot get the job they really want. Negative online behavior is a red flag for any employer. A bitter person who complains about everything cannot collaborate with others or show up on time simply isn't a desirable candidate.

A while back, I noticed that many of my former students posted negative comments on a daily basis, so I decided to conduct a one-month, very unscientific study. From seven to ten in the evening, Monday through Friday, I tabulated their comments and tallied them as negative, positive, or neutral.

> **A little training** in social media etiquette goes **a long way.**

Here were my parameters: Negative comments included posting anger or disappointment toward someone specific, a vague reference (complaining about a job or business that wronged them), or just plain proclaiming that "everything sucks." Comments praising someone (or something), showcasing a good deed, proclaiming they worked, or just welcoming the day in an upbeat way were counted as Positive. Neutral posts were given some leeway. Posts about really bad weather, when it was really bad, or a reaction to a team losing were given a Neutral. Selfie pics were also in some grey area. I gave a positive tally mark for the pics where they were smiling. The "Deuces!" pic in which the subject wasn't not really smiling, or, in most cases, was pouting, were deal breakers, as were all pictures where the subject was flipping the bird. Those were tallied as Negative. If I couldn't decide whether a selfie pic was positive or negative, I just racked them up as Neutral.

After a month of monitoring only former students (ages eighteen to thirty-two) I had approximately 52 percent negative comments, 34 percent neutral, and only 24 percent positive. This study was far from Gallop poll or Pew Research quality, but it gave me a feel for what was being posted on Facebook: negative, angry posts. Yes, I conducted this study during winter, the coldest winter we have had in decades. And yes, I took this poll when unemployment and job dissatisfaction were high. That doesn't change the reality that most of these people were/are using Facebook to vent or as a way to make themselves feel better by posting that everyone else is wrong, messed up, or stupid. When an employer or potential client goes online in search of a bright, collaborative person who will do great work, Facebook is not where these complainers want them to look.

I want my students to consider a much different and better use for social media. My message to them is this: *Imagine an employer's surprise when they see positive messages from the average kid. Better yet, think of the shock when they see you showcase your talents.*

Ponder the advantages for a student with a large network of supporters and followers who provide a source of collaboration or inspiration. Not only will the prospective employer be excited about that student's skill set but also about the potential network the business could tap into by hiring him or her. What the employer expected to be a negative trolling session suddenly transformed into a positive quest of vetting a quality employee. They set out on a mission to find dirt and ended up stumbling upon treasure!

Treat Yourself Like a Professional

My students get used to hearing mantras in class. One they know by heart is, "When you treat yourself like a professional online, everyone else will." Adults, and especially employers, look for reasons to *not* approve of teens. When students post rants, they feed into the self-absorbed, lazy stereotypes and hurt themselves.

A little training in social media etiquette goes a long way. My students know better than to sext, rant, post hate-filled tweets, or share anything else that would get them in trouble. They've learned proper behavior *because* they are encouraged to use social media, especially Twitter, to show off their work. They might slip up once in a while and make a stupid comment but nothing obscene. In fact, when I demonstrate the powerful reach of a tweet or retweet, many of my students end up deleting their previous accounts and starting clean profiles. Their focus becomes attracting and connecting with Twitter all-stars.

Last year, a social-marketing manager from New York, Brian Moran, connected with some of my Innovation Class students. They ended up collaborating with Brian on how to connect with international leaders on Twitter. Brian helped them find a wealth of great connections, and, with more than 150K followers, his re-tweets were gold. My students worked at producing content and writing tweets in hopes that he would retweet their message. They understood that a good network gets projects noticed and can drive traffic to a blog, video, or podcast. By the end of the semester, my students focused exclusively on gaining followers who were professionals or students interested in collaborating.

The funniest part of their quest for social media dominance was the Klout competitions. Klout, if you who don't know, is a service that ranks a person's social influence by studying the interactions on many social media outlets. The rankings go from one to one hundred. Non-celebrities tend to rank in the twenties to thirties, whereas Barak Obama and Justin Bieber rank in the high nineties. The Beibs takes the top spot. (I'll keep my opinions about that to myself.) My students started to compare Klout scores and discovered not all tweets carry the same weight. A retweet from a big name was gold, and a Facebook page post that earned a lot of likes or comments helped to drive up a score. Not only did they want a higher score, but my students also found that being a social influencer became addictive, especially if it was kept professional. My students quickly caught on to the fact that a powerful, inspiring message gets retweeted and liked more than the common rant. Throughout the semester, other students saw how being professional can be cool, and using social media to probe for an honest debate could reflect favorably on them. Pretty soon, adults responded back to them and, even better, asked my students for their insights on various topics.

Birds of a Feather

Students who abuse social media seem to gravitate to the typical social-media bully. They enjoy the thrill of being the first to know some gossip. It's easy for students to get caught up in a tabloid-style craze since entertainment gossip columns and shows like TMZ celebrate gossip and smut. But, if our students are taught to use and even *cherish* social media, they will connect with other motivated students. Indeed, all over the world, there are students who know how to use social media as the ultimate amplification tool. Their knowledge of and respect for the medium separates them from average teens, and they are propelling themselves into social-media stardom.

In the previous chapter, I shared a couple of examples of student-produced videos that earned massive exposure because of the power of social media. The truth is, no other tool can work faster or more inexpensively to bring attention to your students' work. Here are a few more illustrations of how social media can propel the learning experience while increasing your students' networks.

FASHION LOVER FINDS HER VOICE

Anna is a student who learned to use YouTube to connect with fans all over the world. She started by making simple vlogs about fashion and thrift-store finds. Never negative or catty, Anna chose to be bubbly and upbeat. To her surprise, she had ten followers within a month. These girls passed on the YouTube links to other girls via Facebook and Twitter. Pretty soon, she had one hundred subscribers, then two hundred, then a thousand, then two thousand. This network of girls allows her to hear from her fan base, which inspires her to create more videos. She still turns in videos for school, but feedback from her followers probably means more to her now. This is not to say that she isn't working to improve in my class, but her audience members' input gives her ideas that could not come from me. Her creativity is enhanced by hundreds of different sources, and the fact that she owns her platform means she never has to wait for an editor to pass along an assignment.

GOING FOR DISTANCE

Four students in my Innovation Class—Briscon, Grace, Dylan, and Gavin—put together a student-run Massive Open Online Course (MOOC) as an experiment. They wanted to see how quickly they could find and collaborate with networked students. The goal was to create a student version of their go-to site for all things hacked: lifehacker.com. (*Hack* used to mean an unlawful entry into another computer. Today, it means to come up with different solutions, à la *MacGyver*. If you go to lifehacker.com, you will find hacks on everything, from how to jailbreak a smart-

> When high-flying students connect with each other, **magic can happen.**

phone, to how to get rid of fleas on dogs without buying expensive products.)

The group held the opinion that students know quite a bit about technology. With a proper landing site to demonstrate their knowledge, they could exchange ideas for even better hacks. With that vision in mind, they posted messages on Twitter and Google+.

They ended up connecting with a Twitter friend of mine, Verena Roberts. Verena is a distance-learning expert from Canada who specializes in MOOCs. Within a week, my students were collaborating with her as their mentor. They planned the trial run for the project, which included hosting video-based tutorials created by students. A group of thirty interested students were each asked to make a video to explain their talent, or hack, and show how others could accomplish the same task. They were given three weeks to complete their videos.

I would like to tell you we had a bunch of amazing videos come in, but I would be lying. Four videos, all from my students, were posted to the site. Still, neither the group nor myself considered this a failure. Consider what this group's members gained:

1.   They made connections with a large number of educators and students who provided suggestions and/or encouragement.

2.   Their results were typical for MOOCs. According to *The New York Times* writer Tamar Lewin, about ten percent of students finish MOOCs.

3.   The most important lesson was just to start a MOOC and get connected with students who, themselves, were connected. Just like the birds-of-a-feather-flock-together mentality of low-end social gossipers, the highly functioning social-media mavens also flock

together. When they start to connect with each other, magic can happen.

Social Media: The Mentor Resource

Patricia Reagan, a teacher from Canastota, New York, uses Twitter and Facebook to find CEOs for her Apprentice Project. During this ten-week project, students work with, learn from, and are mentored by CEOs from all over the country. She explains:

Students are divided into two teams that compete weekly as they complete tasks assigned by the teacher. The tasks incorporate prior knowledge (in this case marketing theory) to be applied in a real-world scenario. For example, students raise funds for local charities through implementing the marketing mix. Students present the task to a team of judges, consisting of faculty, administration, and local business leaders.

Student teams then meet weekly in the boardroom and discuss the results of the task. The teacher is joined in the boardroom by two advisors (faculty who volunteer for the program) to help guide the meeting and determine strengths and opportunities for improvement. One student is fired and the next task is provided for the following week. After a student is fired, he or she is rehired in a position that best fits the skill sets observed by the teacher. For example, a student is rehired as the public relations director for the program and is responsible for calling media for weekly news updates on the program.

Success of the program is evident as graduates of the program return with stories of truly being hired for the job of their dreams or being accepted into the college of choice. This program directly prepares students for real world tasks, including conference calls, video conferencing, face-to-face sales, boardroom meetings, self-reflection, working in teams, leadership in teams, and countless other soft skills desired in today's workforce.

> ***Students need to connect** with people outside the school walls. The best, **most effective way** to do this is **through social media.***

Sounds great, right? But how did they find their mentors? In addition to simply emailing the prospective mentors, they use Twitter and Facebook to connect with them. Once a relationship is established, weekly Skype meetings give students the opportunity to not simply read about their mentor but talk with them directly.

I met with Patricia two years ago. She'd just implemented the first year of her Apprentice Project. She credited Facebook and Twitter with helping the project's growth and success. I suggested LinkedIn as a potential resource for her quest to find CEOs and other collaborators, but her response made me realize that social media can be less direct and still effective. She explained, "The Apprentice Project has grown so much since I started connecting more on Facebook and Twitter. I often get recommendations or introductions from fellow teachers who are Facebook friends. You know how teachers are: We always know somebody who knows someone else."

Patricia took the I-know-a-guy approach to finding talent on social media. She's discovered, for example, that LinkedIn is most effective when she receives a personal introduction rather than trying to connect to a new person directly. Personally, I think this is genius. Asking a busy CEO out of the blue for his or her time and input is a crap shoot. A businessperson who doesn't know you might not be inclined to hear about the wonderful things your students want to do. Instead, Patricia puts out a request of trusted friends and fellow teachers, who are usually willing to help in the quest of finding collaborative partners. The partnership has a much greater chance of working because, rather than a cold contact, she instantly becomes a familiar face through the warm introduction. Patricia has found that many busy professionals want to give back; the initial approach is when they decide whether they'll agree to help. Having a mutual friend introduce the two parties breaks the ice and adds to the success rate.

Social Media Gets Results— and Scholarships

I share these student and teacher success stories to illustrate a point: Students need to connect with people outside the school walls. *The best, most effective way to do this is through social media.* When they can find enthusiastic professionals and students to work with, truly global collaboration can happen. Beyond the value this medium brings to the classroom, it helps students make connections and create a voice that gets them noticed. Want proof? The real-world experience one of my former students, Brian, took with him to college led to him using social media to find collaborators and showcase video work on YouTube. His videos got noticed and helped him secure internships with *60 Minutes* and *Late Night with Jimmy Fallon* (now known as *The Tonight Show Starring Jimmy Fallon*). He eventually landed a job with NBC's *Today Show.*

Madeleine and Pete, students you'll read more about in Chapter 9, were awarded scholarships because they sought to grow their brand through collaboration and publishing. Madeleine recently graduated from Duke University. Pete is headed to University of Notre Dame on a full ride with an Eli-Lilly Scholarship.

I hope you can see why I'm so passionate about teaching students to use social media for their benefit. Twitter, Facebook, and YouTube are about so much more than what you had for dinner or showing off vacation pictures. They are the way the world connects. They are tools that, when used appropriately, can help students build strong networks and bright futures.

Teach Students to Take Responsibility of Their Digital Brand

As I stated earlier in this chapter, countless people have been denied jobs due to misuse and bad conduct online. Social media has its drawbacks for those who don't take it seriously. However, a proactive approach to correct previous posts can minimize the damage. Ben Honeycutt, a then high school student, started to take his digital branding seriously when he saw how online connections could help him. He did a Google search of his name to make sure his record was clean.

Because Ben gives presentations about leadership and social media etiquette, he knew it was a good idea to check his past online encounters. He was pretty sure nothing would come up, as he used Facebook and Twitter responsibly. However he was surprised to see the Google results once he did a little digging. As an avid sports follower, years of frustration as both a Kansas City Royals and Chiefs fan had gotten the best of him. More than a few of his posts expressed his anger in a not-so-professional way. He was a ticked-off sports fan! In fairness, Ben's posts weren't over the top, but he had dropped a few choice words when his teams lost. If you follow Kansas City sports, know that is a regular occurrence. These posts also were on a forum for sports talk, not on popular social media sites, thus his offenses were not too daunting. Because he wanted to protect himself from criticism later, he was proactive and wrote to the webmaster about getting his posts off the site. I'm sure the webmaster got a chuckle, but Ben explained he was thinking about his future and didn't want a couple of choice quotes to define him later.

> *Twitter, Facebook, and YouTube are **tools** that can **help students build strong networks** and **bright futures.***

We have all made dumb comments that we later regret. But I am glad Ben learned to value his digital brand enough to recognize that his words could come back to haunt him. Wiping them off the record was the smart thing to do. That said, his example is a hard one to replicate; Ben's problem was easy to fix, comparatively speaking. (Many people have more than just a couple of sports-related rants.) What I love about Ben's story is that it shows students *can* grasp the importance of social media as a tool that should be used and respected.

In the next chapter, we will talk about the basics: what to post—and what *never* to post—how to set up successful Twitter profiles and Facebook groups, and how to use these tools effectively.

quick thoughts

- Social Media can be dangerous, which is why training is so important.

- Training on the benefits of social media is often overshadowed by rules of what not to do.

- Students (and adults) too often use social media to complain and rant.

- Imagine the advantage when employers and college admission officers see talents and great work on display.

- A strong professional network can help point you and your students to success.

- Deleting old accounts, or cleaning up posts and taking responsibility for past negative transgressions are steps in the right direction.

notes

7

GETTING STARTED WITH SOCIAL MEDIA

By now, I hope you understand why I love social media as a tool for learning. Just to be sure we're on the same page, here's a quick recap. Social media provides:

- Students with opportunities to collaborate with other students.

- Educators with opportunities to learn from and encourage other teachers.

- Students and educators with opportunities to discuss ideas with mentors from the community and around the world.

- Students and educators with opportunities to share their projects and best practices.

Are you seeing a theme? Social media has the power to amplify the learning experience by *providing opportunities to create and collaborate* with people, companies and communities—globally.

If you are a teacher or parent, I know you want your students to have the best opportunities. If you are a student, this is the way to stand above the rest. So even if you aren't completely convinced that social media is the way to go, let me make a recommendation: Try it. You don't have to commit for a lifetime. Commit for a term, a school year. Consider it an experiment.

If you are ready to step, even temporarily, into the world of social media, *congratulations*! In this chapter, I'll show you how to create your profile and take part in groups and chats. I'll also share some of the Dos and Don'ts for social media. But first, I want to talk about the different types of social media users: Hawks, Crows, and Owls.

Hawks, Crows, and Owls

Three different types of users make up the social media community. I will use Twitter to illustrate my point, but you can apply these truths to any platform. First, there's the **Hawk**, the A-List celebrity, be it a rock star or a rock-star teacher. This user's posts usually involve their opinions. He or she has lots of followers, some good insights, and doesn't follow people back. I call these users hawks, because like the bird, they are top-tier, admired, self-sufficient, and independent. It is rare to see a kettle (aka flock) of hawks because they do not need help hunting and don't seem to like companionship outside of their mates.

Hawks usually post things about themselves. They do not retweet too much, nor do they respond back when you tweet at them. Some might think of this as arrogance, while others believe that they are simply too busy to answer. For example, A-List celebrity Katy Perry has millions of followers and follows less than two hundred. She posts about her upcoming appearances, daily life, and various other personal insights. If you tweet a message to her, it is highly unlikely that she will respond back. Few would say this lack of response implies arrogance; rather, people tend to understand that the volume of messages and the rigors of her celebrity schedule consume her time.

Hawks exist in education as well. Thought leader Sir Ken Robinson is a good example. After his TED talk in 2006, Robinson became a celebrity to many of us in education. At the time of this book's printing, he had more than 250,000 Twitter followers but followed fewer than 700 people. Because Robinson doesn't sing, appear in movies, or excel in a sport, some might not consider him a celebrity. However, in the educational realm, he is a superstar who is likely inundated with tweets and messages. If he doesn't respond to all those messages, it isn't a matter of arrogance; he simply doesn't have the time.

Local hawks, however, are another story. A local hawk is the all-star teacher in your town or school building. This person is the teacher who posts examples of their class's work on social media

*Even if you aren't completely convinced social media is the way to go, **try it.** You don't have to commit for a lifetime.*

and or passes along interesting articles. What makes this person a hawk is his or her one-way communication and tendency not to follow back.

If you are a teacher, make a point to follow back teachers. That is not to say that you have to follow everyone who follows you. But at a minimum, follow the educators and people who are passionate about education who follow you. If you don't, you risk sending the message that other people's opinions don't count. Flying alone may work if you have a hit album or have been knighted by the Queen of England, but it doesn't work well for teachers.

Educators who are willing to follow other teachers and engage in dialogue are **Crows**. Crows are highly intelligent animals who enjoy social interaction with the flock. In terms of social media, crows tend to have a more balanced following and follower numbers. Again, as a crow, you don't have to follow everyone back. You may choose to follow back only other crows, people who will engage in a two-way discussion about education-related topics.

I like crows best because they provide a wealth of information. The downside of all that communication is that your Twitter wall gets busy when you follow more than 1,000 people. The answer to that problem is Twitter *lists*. Lists allow you to sort or segment the people you follow into

> *Flying alone may work if you have a hit album or have been knighted by the Queen of England, but it **doesn't work well for teachers.***

groups. This lets you focus your attention. For example, I might want to read about educational technology one night. If I find some key teachers who use *EdTech* tools well, I can make a list called EdTech All Stars. My list may have only twenty users, making it very manageable to review. This is also why I like it when teachers identify their educational interests in their profile descriptions. For example, I'll automatically sort someone whose profile reads, "Teacher passionate about Augmented Reality," into a Twitter list with others who are interested in that field, educators like Drew Minock and Brad Waid (@TechMinock and @TechBradWaid).

Just like the bird, social media crows enjoy engaging and chatting, so keep it light. Sharing professional insights is great, but keeping a fun demeanor is helpful. Also, avoid making negative statements about education, your job, and especially your students. I've already mentioned how negative talk can harm your reputation. It's also a fast way to lose followers and respect.

Lastly, there are **Owls**. This group likes to observe and gain wisdom from others but is usually quiet and doesn't mind being alone. I used to call this group stealers, because they glean ideas from other teachers without posting their own. The reality is that almost all great teachers steal ideas; we just call it borrowing best practices. Owls usually follow a smaller number of educators and enjoy reading about new trends or techniques. Having a lot of followers is not a priority with an owl, so engaging in dialogue isn't that important to them. My owl friends often say they are too busy to join in chats and prefer to hunt for tweets pointing them to great educational resources.

Generally speaking, teachers tend to be owls that follow fewer than fifty people and are followed back by fewer than ten. They might be on social media so they can follow an administrator or fellow teacher at their school or they just want to see what all the fuss is about. This silent majority is a powerful group. Even though they don't post a lot or talk back and forth, they harness the power of social media for themselves and their students.

As you get started with your personal social media experience, or experiment, realize that it's perfectly fine to be an owl. As you get more comfortable with the platform, challenge yourself to engage with other innovative educators. The more you contribute, the more you'll learn and grow. Now, let's get started with some basics.

First Things First: Set Up Your User Profile

Every social media platform requires you to create a user profile. The following rules for setting up a profile apply to any social media platform, be it Twitter, Facebook, Instagram, Google+, Pinterest, etc.

Your first task is to choose a username. Let me warn you, cute usernames do not scream professionalism in education. Avoid usernames like *VegasGirl65*, or *HugeColtsFan72*. If possible, stick to your name or a variation of it. My user name is *DonWettrick*.

Next, you will need to fill out your profile information. This is a brief description of yourself. Again my recommendation is to keep it professional and relevant.

Don't do this:

Don Wettrick
Colts fan. Lover of hot sauce. Father of three. Master of none.
Indianapolis, IN   www.theinnovationteacher.com

While factual, this type of profile is bad because educators do not care about my sports teams or my love of hot sauce. The father of three part is fine, but if my primary objective is to connect with educators, then I need to make that clear on my profile.

A better profile looks something like this:

Don Wettrick
Passionate educator who enjoys using social media to connect.
EdTech enthusiast. Father of three.
Innovation Coordinator at Noblesville HS
Indianapolis, IN www.theinnovationteacher.com

If you want to use Twitter for education, make sure your profile says either something about education or the fact that you are a teacher. If you are a student looking to connect with professionals, list that in your profile! My second profile example tells other users about my interests in education. There may still be room for a hobby, but my goal is to engage with professional educators, not hot sauce fans. The priority is to include the topic about which you want to connect with other people.

One final note on setting up your profile: Show your face. Few people want to follow a picture of an egg or a missing man. *Please*, post a decent photo of you. Select a picture—formal or candid, as long as it doesn't discredit your professionalism in any way—and crop it so that your face is clearly visible. I can't tell you how many times people stop me at a conference to say hello because they recognize me from my profile picture. It's a great icebreaker and allows people to put a face with a tweet… uh… name.

Build Your Professional Learning Network

Next, start following, or friending, a few people. With Facebook, you have to wait for the other user to follow you back, which is why I like Twitter better for gaining immediate insight on professional development. As soon as you follow someone on Twitter, you can see his or her posts. I am often asked, "How do I know whom to follow?" When you set up an account for the first time, Twitter and Facebook will give you recommendations based on your email address book. However, unless you already have their contact information, those sites won't automatically suggest great educational leaders. You'll learn as you go how to find people to follow. In fact, I think learning the nuances of social media should be done by self-discovery, but here are a few tips to help you get started.

> **Show your face.** Few people want to follow a picture of an egg or missing man.

1. Follow close friends and fellow teachers/co-workers and see whom they follow.

2. Search for the names of people who've influenced you: authors or speakers, for example.

3. Look for people who have similar interests. (See below.)

Monitoring educational hashtags is an excellent way to find people who care about the same things you do. Do a Google search on popular educational hashtags, like #EdChat, #EdTech, and #Elearning. I highly suggest participating in group chats, denoted by the aforementioned hashtags. Some chat groups, like #EdChat, include people from all across the United States and around the world. Others are quite local, like #InELearning (Indiana E Learning) or #MillerShift (my high school's chat hashtag). If you want to gain knowledge or just see what these groups are talking about, type one of these hashtags into the search feature at the top of the page on Twitter. Keeping up with chats can be difficult if they are moving fast. To make it a little easier, check out TweetDeck or HootSuite. These applications allow you to watch a live stream of tweets as they come across with the hashtag that you are monitoring in real time.

Group pages are the Facebook alternative to Twitter's hashtag chats. Facebook has a much easier system of following along and monitoring conversations within niche groups. I mentioned earlier that tweets are

> *Don't be deterred by a group's private label; if you're interested, **request to join.***

limited to 140 characters, so the chats often point the reader to a blog link or other site for more information. Facebook's posts don't have that limit, so they can go into more depth right there on the group page.

Most groups are public, so you can join and instantly see posts and article recommendations. I recommend Facebook pages like Edutopia, ASCD, or ISTE. Because some people like to post only negative comments or conduct themselves in an abusive manner, some group managers make their pages private. This only means that users have to ask to join and be approved. Don't be deterred by the *private* label; if you're interested, request to join. Some group pages are private because they are intended to be a smaller setting. My favorite groups are from smaller conferences I've attended. They are kept private because the setting was intimate, and the discussions center on the specific content of the event.

Make a Core Group of Friends

After you've monitored a few groups or Twitter chats, join in! Start to dialogue with your fellow teachers, gain some insight, and ask for some guidance. Almost all of the educators I have met online are more than helpful. Your discussions can lead to great friendships and can help you grow professionally. Even if your first core group of friends or followers can't provide the information you're looking for, someone from the group will most likely be able to point you to other resources.

I mentioned earlier that I started my Twitter account at a conference. The first people I followed and the first to follow me back were at the conference. Then, some of the friends of the conference attendees started to follow me as well. One person who really stands out as someone who helped me learn the ropes on Twitter is Ian Adair. Ian, a non-profit specialist at the Martinez Foundation, reached out to me on Twitter because a friend attended the same conference and saw my tweets. During the following six months he gave me suggestions on who to follow and popular hashtags to explore. He also sent my name out in #FF (Friday Follow) recommendation tweets to his followers. Suddenly, I had twenty more interesting followers from Ian's network following me, and, more importantly, we were sharing information and insights.

One Friday, I decided to follow the other names included in Ian's #FF tweet. I was particularly interested in one follower, Dave Guymon, because he had just self-published his own book, *If You Can't Fail, It Doesn't Count.* I wanted his insights on education and how social media had impacted his teaching. Like Ian, he shared information with me and made introductions to other great educators and professionals from whom I could learn. In fact, Dave also shared how he met a fellow educator on Twitter who became his book editor! Even more incredibly, the two didn't meet face-to-face before the book was published. To me, this sort of networking and collaboration are the ultimate reasons to connect on social media.

What Would Your Mom Think?

For all the excellent benefits of social media, there are a few things I want to caution you to remember. First and foremost, think before you post. Ask yourself before posting anything, "What would my mom think?" Better yet, just have your mother follow you! I know it helps me. I've had a few Facebook posts questioned by my mom and dad. Knowing they read my posts makes me think twice about what I write.

Also, avoid political comments, especially negative comments. While you might think your side is right and the other party is stupid, when you post political comments, especially those that convey those sentiments, you cut down chances to collaborate with other teachers by half. Political rants do not attract teachers who want to collaborate. You could offend a great teacher who would have worked with you had he or she not read your angry posts. If you are a great teacher, I do not care if you are a Republican, Democrat, Libertarian, Green Party, Independent, or if you just plain hate politics. I am on social media to learn about best practices and share what works for my students. While I might not like some policies that come out of the political process, I choose not to use social media as a place to engage in negative dialogue. I'll get my information from trusted news sources, not from an angry Twitter user. In fact, I usually opt out of Facebook pages or unfollow people who post overly negative comments or constantly complain about politics. A few notorious educational Facebook groups constantly discuss politics. Angry political posts and nasty arguments are the norm there. Looking over the posts in these groups, you'll see mostly division, and few, if any, usable techniques. My advice: Opt out of those groups. Yes, political debates are important; we need to voice differing opinions if we're going to see changes. But, for teachers who want to change what goes on in the classroom, social media isn't the place to constantly complain about politics.

Be smart about who you follow and friend. I told you that my personal policy is not to follow current students on Facebook. One of my reasons for this is that, in some districts, teachers can be fired for following students on social media. Better to be safe than sorry. Before you follow students on any social media platform, please get written permission from your administration. Review school policy about acceptable Internet use before you interact with students online.

Do not complain about your job on social media. I am always amazed by news stories reporting that a teacher was fired because of something he or she posted Facebook or Twitter. Most employment terminations, however, result because of negative comments teachers have made about their students. Educators are mini-celebrities in the community. When teachers post something negative about their students, they will receive *negative* attention, sometimes in the form of a pink slip. In the same vein, don't post negative comments about your school, administration, or other teachers. It's just a bad idea, not to mention, it's unprofessional. Even if you have a valid point about a problem within your school, social media is not the place to air the dirty laundry. Sure, you have the right to free speech… as long as you're willing to accept the consequences.

Lastly, remember that your comments are forever. People and situations change, but your digital legacy is permanent. I see just as many adults as students abusing social media. Because social media is a relatively new phenomenon, many users are just now figuring out how damaging negative posts can be. Use common sense and think before you post. Constantly remind yourself to keep your digital legacy positive. Remember,

Be smart *about who you follow and friend.* **Review school policy** *about acceptable Internet use before you interact with students online.*

your current and future employers will be looking at your digital past. Make sure it's positive!

Get Out There!

In my original draft of this chapter, I went into too much detail about Twitter jargon, trends, and how to use Twitter lists and Tweet Deck. Then, I realized that getting started on social media is deeply personal. Much like learning anything of value, one must learn by self-discovery. I have laid out some of the very basic steps, but getting out there and being a hawk, crow, or owl is what it is really about.

My PLN (professional learning network) has helped me become a much better teacher. I get more information from more sources. Social media has given me the power to try new things and provide feedback that may prevent someone else from making my mistakes. It also has allowed me the opportunity to teach social media studies to my students. They know the power it holds, and I can honestly say that my students are better digital citizens because we have learned together. Thus, the suggestions in this chapter on how to craft a social media account also apply to your students as well.

If you haven't already, I encourage you to create a Facebook or Twitter account and start learning and sharing. If you don't know whom to follow, I would be honored to be your first follow. If you are a teacher or express an interest in education, I will follow back! If your students want to follow me, I would be even more honored!

quick thoughts

- There are three different types of users on social media: Hawks, Crows, and Owls. Hawks post a lot but do not follow back. Crows are social and like to engage in dialogue. Owls are quiet and usually don't follow too many people. Regardless of your engagement level, follow back fellow educators.

- Select a simple, direct profile name for your account. Your name is usually sufficient.

- Start following a core group of people who share your values. Get to know the jargon and join in discussions... or at least follow the discussions.

- Think before you post! Keep politically charged and negative comments to yourself!

- Embrace social media to help propel innovation.

- Spread your wings and fly!

notes

8

OPPORTUNITIES ARE EVERYWHERE

Teachers know everybody. That's why some teachers go into real estate or local politics. We know someone or have a friend that knows someone. We're mini-celebrities in our communities, which is exactly why I *know* opportunities are everywhere.

The way I see it, we have two choices in light of today's economy: We can bemoan smaller budgets and lack of resources, or we can put our I-know-somebody power to work. That is what this chapter is all about, and it is an important component of any Innovation Class project.

Through the years, I have been amazed at the number of times when I've only had to ask for what I needed. Sometimes, I ask via Twitter or Facebook (we've talked about that already). Other times, I look at my network, the people in my community.

Case in point: I live just outside of Indianapolis, Indiana. In February 2012, our city hosted Super Bowl XLVI. When the NFL announced it would open up the media day to the public, it was music to the ears of almost everyone in my broadcasting class. We could pay for a ticket and talk to the players... so we thought. We bought six tickets to the event, but after reading the fine print, it turned out that we would be seated and equipped with a closed circuit radio so we could listen to the media ask questions. Not as exciting, but we had already bought the tickets.

After learning about the restricted access, two of the students didn't really want to go. I told them that, if we went, packed our camera equipment, and acted like professionals, success would find us. Two of my favorite mantras are "Opportunities are everywhere" and "If you treat yourself like a professional, others will too." The plan was to show up, interview as many people outside the event, and earn our way in as real media professionals.

We packed our cameras, tripods, wireless microphones, dressed like reporters, and set out on our journey. As soon as we arrived, we started interviewing anyone who would talk to us: the event volunteers, police officers, sports fans, and locals just taking in the scene. Then we saw our first opportunity: A local Fox affiliate was broadcasting a live morning show just outside the stadium. We asked to get interviews, and they graciously accepted. My reporter, Tyler, grabbed the mic and started asking good open-ended questions. After we wrapped up, we asked if they had an extra pass to get into the media day event. Their response was, "Sorry kid, we don't have them ourselves; we only got a couple for our sports guys and lead anchors."

We thanked them and saw opportunity number two: *Mike and Mike in the Morning* on ESPN was broadcasting live a block over. Quickly, we packed up our equipment and hustled over to the ESPN booth. By this time, we had only one hour before the gates opened for media day.

At the ESPN booth, my student, Brad, and I approached one of the producers and asked if we could get an interview with one of the two Mikes during a commercial break. "I'll see what I can do," he said in a tone that told us he wasn't interested in giving us the time of day, much less an interview. Another student, Emily, boldly asked, "Are you going to get them now?" The producer again acted busy and turned away, pretending to talk to someone on his headset.

Now we were twenty minutes to opening.

I told them that we should pack it up and head for the stadium for our seats but to be on the lookout for *any* good opportunity. "Just keep looking," I told them. That's when I saw a short African American man wearing a nice trench coat and Stetson hat. I immediately recognized the man.

I pointed to Tyler and said, "Go get him."

"Who the heck is that guy?" Tyler asked. "I don't think he is an athlete."

I told him it was DeMorris Smith, the NFL's Player Association President. Earlier that month, I had watched a *60 Minutes* episode on the NFL lockout and how Smith had saved the season.

Tyler caught up to Smith, who was on his way to the entry gate, and politely tapped him on the shoulder. "Excuse me, Mr. Smith, I would like to ask you a few questions."

Mr. Smith kept walking. Without breaking stride, he replied, "Sorry, I'm not doing interviews today."

Then magic happened. Tyler played the school kid role. It reminded me of the Mean Joe Green Coca-Cola television ad with the kid tugging on the heartstrings. "I'm just a student, sir. I would like to get an interview with you for my school."

He stopped in his tracks, turned around, and saw five well-dressed students, a teacher, and a professional looking camera set-up. "I would love to do an interview," he told us. He said something to his assistant and then proceeded to do a ten-minute interview with a fifteen-year-old student. Tyler started off very nervous but gained confidence with each passing question. He wisely began with softball questions about how Smith had saved the season from the strike and how Indianapolis was fairing as host of the Super Bowl week. Then Tyler asked some tougher questions about labor conditions and, most importantly to Indianapolis Colts fans: What would happen to Peyton Manning? At the end of the interview, Tyler thanked

> *Teachers know **everybody**, which is exactly why I know **opportunities are everywhere.***

> When you **ask for help**, you'll find that the overwhelming majority of **people are excited** about **helping students succeed.**

Smith, shook hands, and tried to contain his open-mouthed smile of wild amazement about what just happened.

Then the "opportunities are everywhere" mantra really came to fruition. Smith turned and introduced himself to me and complimented me on my students' professionalism. "I'm really impressed with your students. When you get inside, find me. I'll get you an interview with anyone you want. Tom, Eli, Justin... you name it." As it occurred to me that *Tom* was Brady, *Eli* was Manning, and *Justin* was Tuck, I stood momentarily speechless. Just as I was about to let him walk away, I came to my senses.

"Sir, we don't have media credentials; we just brought six tickets and some hope." After a long pause, he reached into his wallet and pulled out his business card.

"You do now," he said handing me the card. "Go check in and have them call me. I'll make sure you get in."

Keeping Watch

I share that story for several reasons. First, it was a memorable day. I mean it was Super Bowl media day! I could tell endless stories about my student interviewing Teddy Brusci, our mayor, or having ESPN's Chris Berhman cutting promos for our school's announcements. (Seriously, I could write an entire book about this *one* day.) But the real reason I brought up this experience is to demonstrate what happens when you actively look for opportunities. I have had several similar moments, although not as monumental, when I was determined to find money, partnerships, or help for my students. The reality is, whether it's by connecting on Twitter, making a vlog on YouTube, or striking up a conversation at an airport, I am always watching for opportunities for my students.

As teachers, we know so many people—or know people who know people. Why not intentionally tug on a few heartstrings and pull Tyler's "I'm just a student" routine? Despite broad stroke, negative press from the media, most people actually love teachers and are willing to help in all sorts of ways. Yes, education is criticized as a whole, but when it comes to individual schools or teachers, community support remains strong. When you ask for help, you'll find that the overwhelming majority of people are excited about helping students succeed. But you have to ask… with passion and urgency.

When I open myself up to opportunities to meet people, I am always thinking about how a person's expertise or job can enhance my students' careers or learning experiences. If they have an interesting job, I want to have a student produce a short documentary about them. Or if they run a not-for-profit group that needs publicity, I make sure we partner with them. Helping others always helps us. Not only do we get a great experience, but we also benefit from the power of networking.

For example, each year I run a county-wide film festival at a historic theater. A few years ago, I formed a partnership with the theater to show films produced by high school students. It's great, not only for the filmmakers who get to see their films on a big screen, but also for the community members who enjoy the festival. As an added bonus, the public gets to see firsthand the quality of work high school students are capable of producing.

Two years ago, *The Indianapolis Star* featured an article on the festival and how the films impacted the local community and boosted student moral. After writing the article, the reporter for *The Indy Star* ® called me at school. "Your students are talented," he said. "Those films weren't just good for students; they were good, period." After discussing the students' skill and creativity, we came up with an idea for a partnership between my broadcasting students and *The Indy Star* ®. Many newspapers today use video content in their web editions. He suggested that two students could film and produce a 90-second video while Vic, the writer, conduct-ed an interview. Our students would gain experience, as well as exposure, to real news, and The Indy Star® would have access to free, quality video content.

Our second assignment for The Indy Star® was to shoot video about a local business that designed and manufactured a very popular scooter called the Rockboard Scooter. During the filming, the owner asked about our video experience. I bragged a bit on my students and told him we had produced two commercials for area businesses. He inquired further about our equipment, price, and dedication. I assured him that we could indeed make a nice thirty-second commercial for him. What he didn't tell me is that it was not for a little market like the south side of Indianapolis. It was for Southern California! It turned out that Toys"R"Us® was selling the scooters online—as was Amazon and Walmart—and they wanted an advertisement to test the market from San Diego to Los Angeles.

Talk about an educational experience! I will never forget the first screening we did with the owner for the commercial. He loved it but had a few suggestions for improvements. He also questioned whether the commercial would be completed on time. Phil, the student manager, assured him the team would meet the deadline. When the owner told us how much he had already spent on time slots for the Los Angeles area, our jaws hit the floor. We were stunned, not as much by the cost as by the fact that this business owner took such a huge risk trusting five fifteen- to seventeen-year-old students to complete a daunting and important task for his company.

I am happy to report that the commercial went well. Did it look like a professional commercial? Not exactly professional; it was nicer than a typical local car dealer's ad but not as nice as a Ford commercial. But the client was pleased, and, most importantly, our students produced every-thing: the script, the shots, graphics, and even the background music. How many Midwest US students can claim they shot a commercial that aired in California?

Our opportunities grew from a partnership with a local theater, to an inquiry about working with a local newspaper, to the chance to make a commercial for a major market. The point is, you won't know what opportunities are out there until you actively start looking for them. If you're open to them, sometimes opportunities *find you*. When that happened to me, my perspective on innovation and the impact it can have on students' lives forever changed.

> *You won't know what **opportunities are out there** until you actively **start looking** for them.*

Obesity in Innovation

I have a 500-pound student. I'm stating this up front not to shock you, but to get it out of the way. Eric was overweight and depressed; there is no other way to put it. But things are changing in Eric's life and in several of my other students' lives as well. Let me explain.

Within the first week of school, I noticed that Eric was extremely withdrawn. He hid by going about his business in a very quiet way and not talking to anyone. Unfortunately, his weight became an issue within that first week as well. On the second day of class, his desk broke. I had to explain to him that a chair would be provided for him because the desks couldn't handle his size. As we talked, I invited him to walk with me before school for a little exercise. While he didn't accept my offer—he had no transportation to school other than the school bus—he seemed comfortable in talking to me about his situation.

A couple of weeks passed and something both awkward and serendipitous happened. Eric had not showered for several days, and he looked defeated. When the class broke up into groups, I quietly pulled him into the hallway for a private talk. It was a moment I will cherish for the rest of my life.

As we addressed his situation, he admitted that he didn't care—about anything. He made it abundantly clear that he was depressed and had given up. He understood that he was going to face many health concerns

> **Excellence** *is what results when students and teachers* **collaborate!**

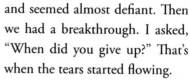

and seemed almost defiant. Then we had a breakthrough. I asked, "When did you give up?" That's when the tears started flowing.

We both stood in the hallway, crying, as he explained that his dad had passed away three years ago. Tired of being ridiculed and picked on for his weight and still grieving for his dad, Eric believed it was easier to not care about anything. Finally, I said, "I can't just sit here and watch this happen; I have to help." I again offered to come in early and start walking with him in the mornings, or after school, and again he explained that he didn't have transportation. Then a light bulb went off in my head. Earlier in the day, an Innovation Class student named Kevin told me he was on the lookout for a new project.

When you're actively looking for opportunities, they find you. I asked if Kevin was up for the challenge of helping Eric; he was more than excited. We devised a plan where Eric would come to my class and work with Kevin. You see, Kevin was looking for an innovation project that could truly help someone in need. We had both read John Medina's *Brain Rules* and learned that simple exercise, like walking, not only improves heart health but brain function as well. In fact, when we need ideas for our Innovation Class, we take walk-and-talks to help spark our creativity. Kevin hypothesized that a simple walking routine would help Eric's health as well as his grades.

Because every Innovation project requires students to collaborate with outside experts, Kevin scheduled a meeting with a dietitian and wellness specialist from a local hospital. The boys worked out a plan together based on what Kevin learned. Eric agreed to keep a food log of everything he ate in a day. This practice made him more aware of his food choices and how often he ate. Kevin and Eric also began walking together almost two hours a day. Within the first two weeks, Eric lost almost ten pounds. But the story doesn't end there. In fact, it only gets better.

When another student, Tessa, overheard Kevin and me talking about the project, she asked whether she could be a part of this experiment. With a background similar to Eric's, she felt she could not only benefit from the extra exercise, but could be a friend to Eric as well. When Tessa joined the club, another Innovation student, Grace, asked to participate as a female mentor for Tessa. Kevin and Grace are popular students for all the right reasons: good grades, kind hearts, good athletes, etc. While they've always been compassionate, they said this experience has helped them become even more aware of students who are in need of some kindness.

Meanwhile, another teacher, Lesleigh Groce, got involved by inviting two more students to join our little club. Groce teaches a foods and nutrition class that fits perfectly with the project's focus on wellness. Together, the students are doing more than walking; they are learning about healthy food alternatives, active lifestyles, and how to create overall happiness. To take it one step further, Groce applied for grant money to purchase various health aids and even healthy food alternatives to encourage healthier eating. Put simply, Lesleigh Groce jumped in and made this project even bigger and better and opened this club to more students. She even got Jared Fogle, Subway's spokesman, to visit the school and talk to the walking club. Excellence is what results when students and teachers collaborate!

The most important and exciting outcome of this Innovation project is that these students are happier! While I'm pleased about Eric and Tessa's weight loss, I am moved to tears watching Kevin and Grace develop these relationships. Meaningful friendships have formed. No longer trying to hide from the world, Eric asked if we could start doing weekly YouTube updates. Tessa began publishing her poetry, and, soon, her art on Grace's blog, which artistically lays out her transformation. I cannot imagine how many students she might impact by their willingness to share their journey!

I was grateful that the school allowed us to seize this opportunity. I especially appreciated Lesleigh Groce's willingness to adjust her schedule. Yes, we had to clear student participation with the parents, and, yes, we had to write a waiver, but it was totally worth it! I hope Ms. Groce can continue this walking club for several years to come!

Untapped Resources

The examples above show how teachers and students can easily find excellent projects and opportunities at school. Collaboration can and should include looking beyond the school walls. Encouraging students to get out into the world and connect with people empowers them to have real, meaningful, even *life-changing* experiences. I tell my students and other teachers: Put down your cell phone, strike up a conversation, and relate to people. Look for needs to fill and problems to solve. Opportunities are everywhere for students and for you as an educator. Get excited about actively seeking out people and asking them to aid you in your students' education. I promise you'll get more *Yes* responses than rejections.

As I have mentioned before, there is a fine, but important, line between a teacher finding great collaborators and mentors and pointing students in the right direction. A stronger bond forms when the students find their own mentors. By encouraging your students to find great mentors, you empower them to find their own opportunities. And I believe that's our job: equipping students to find opportunities and own their education. When your students learn to think and work for themselves, you will have opened a vast, untapped resource.

This past summer, I encouraged the students who pre-enrolled in my class for the next school year to use the summer break to find great opportunities to serve, learn and grow. And I challenged them to look for potential collaborators. Using tools like my blog and YouTube to create the content, I explained the assignment. (Actually, the assignment was open to any and all teachers and students.) The parameters were to find great opportunities, whether it be helping a lady take her groceries to her car, volunteering at a blood drive, or connecting with an expert in an interesting field. Once a connection is made, tweet about the experience and include the hashtag #OAEproj, which stands for "Opportunities Are Everywhere Project." Within days, students posted pictures on Instagram and Twitter of people they had met, opportunities they'd found, and collaborators willing to help in future projects. While it pleased me that my students had made some great contacts, I felt even happier knowing that they were learning to engage intentionally with people. The biggest surprise came when I received feedback from a church in Northern California, explaining that they showed my YouTube video in their service and encouraged their congregation to get out and serve!

Looking to add value to the world by volunteering your time is a gift to yourself. The relation-

Encouraging **students** *to get out into the world and* **connect** *with people* **empowers** *them to have meaningful, even* **life-changing experiences.**

ships, connections, and life lessons that came out of the #OAEproj were priceless. If my Innovation Class students only learn how to connect with others and look to serve, I'll be happy.

The next chapter includes stories from a few students who have experienced the benefits of passion-based, student-designed Innovation projects. I wanted you to hear from their point of view. Each story demonstrates the power of students who are encouraged by their teachers, schools and parents to follow their passions.

quick thoughts

- Teachers can find opportunities by simply engaging with local community members and talking about what is going on in their class. Sometimes, it's as easy as asking for assistance.

- Being on the lookout for great experiences usually leads to success.

- Training our students how to look for opportunities is a skill worth teaching.

- One of the biggest, untapped resources our schools possess is students finding their own collaborators and projects. The teacher doesn't always have to find the next lesson or experience!

- Using social media to promote student collaboration might inspire others to action. You don't know how far the ripples reach out, so promote and inspire!

notes

9

STUDENT VOICES

So far, I've shared my experiences and those of other teachers. In this chapter, I want to let you hear from students who embody the innovation spirit. Four of the five featured students did not take an Innovation Class, yet they found opportunities to push the boundaries and take responsibility for their education. With all the disparaging talk we hear about kids today, it's rare that we ever hear from the students themselves, seek their input, or listen to their insights. This is your chance. I hope you'll be as inspired by their stories and excitement for learning and living as I am. If you would like to read more success stories about student innovators, I highly recommend *Creating Innovators* in which Tony Wagner chronicles the habits and backgrounds of creative, successful students.

From Student to CEO

Paige Woodard
FORMER INNOVATION CLASS STUDENT
FRANKLIN COMMUNITY HIGH SCHOOL, FRANKLIN, INDIANA

When I enrolled in the Innovation class my senior year and I was given free rein to decide what I would learn for the year, I was intimidated. In today's education system, students rarely possess the ability to make decisions in regard to personalizing their education beyond the ability to choose whether to make a colorful poster or an animated PowerPoint presentation for an assignment. Like many of my classmates, I entered Mr. Wettrick's Innovation class without any idea about what I would focus on throughout the year.

Luckily, Mr. Wettrick was prepared for this roadblock and had already prepared a great speech to motivate us into thinking like an innovator. In fact, one of the greatest aspects of Innovation was the weekly brainstorming sessions in which each student would present ideas to the class for discussion. Through this method, I chose my topic of interest within the first week of school: social media in the education system.

If one were asked to list the top priorities of a teenager in the twenty-first century, maintaining communication with friends on social media sites, such as Twitter, Facebook, and Instagram, would probably be at the top of the list. How students communicate on social media networking sites and what they post is often a misuse of the true power of social media. Social media is used in the professional world for networking and collaborating with individuals all over the world. My mission became educating the educators on the benefits of social media in the classroom, the consequences for students who abuse its power, and how it can be incorporated into the curriculum.

My own professional networking on social media led to me delivering a presentation at Stanford University, thanks to my mentor Howard Rheingold, author and adjunct professor specializing in modern communications and technology. I ended up starting my own business,

Education Media Tools Inc., and producing my "Social Networks, Educator Empowerment, and Student Success" DVD. I also received a nomination for the Bammy Awards 2014 in Student Voice. These great successes were accomplished in just seven months after enrolling in the Innovation class and using social media for professional purposes.

Mentors played a huge role in my success. In addition to Howard Rheingold, my mentors included Eric Sheninger, principal at New Milford High School in New Jersey, and our teacher, Don Wettrick. These individuals, as well as numerous others, are passionate about my social media education mission and wanted to help propel my project forward with full force. They set up interviews, advertised my mission on Twitter, and provided invaluable advice on how to make a name for myself in the education world. These educators also contributed content to my DVD and invited others to buy it as an instructional guide for incorporating social media in the classroom.

For me, the greatest advantage of participating in the Innovation Class my senior year was the variety of skills I gained from the experience. Before embarking on a journey to create a DVD to educators, I was clueless on how to film and produce a video or how to upload it to YouTube. Therefore, I began my project with a ten-episode series titled, "The Top Ten Things Not to Do on Twitter" and created my own YouTube channel. Though these videos are basic and (with the top of my head cropped out of some), they gave me a taste of what it was like to speak in

> "I learned how to **stand up** for myself, **stay confident in my beliefs**, **balance** a busy schedule, and maintain a **professional** persona even when I really wanted to act like a teenager."
> —*Paige Woodard*

front of a camera and built my confidence up enough to openly and passionately discuss my opinions in front of an audience. These newly acquired skills benefited me when I was interviewing educators through Skype or Google+ Hangouts in preparation for my DVD. They paid off again when I was interviewed on live Hangouts for a few educational web series.

With those skills, I learned how to stand up for myself, stay confident in my beliefs, balance a busy schedule, maintain a professional persona even when I really wanted to act like a teenager, and, most importantly, I learned what it takes to create a brand for myself. Furthermore, I developed my brand into a potential career, created my own business, and spoke to numerous professionals about everything from opening up a bank account, creating and copyrighting a logo, and learned what it means to be a digital citizen and role model.

In just nine months, I learned a lot about what it means to be a professional and found my niche in business. All thanks to the experience I had in the Innovation class, I am on my way to becoming a successful businesswoman. Specifically, this journey helped prepare me for the trials I will face throughout my career in business and provided me with the tools to overcome them. Though I am still young and will make countless mistakes in my lifetime, I will always have the skills and tools I gained in the Innovation class to fall back on.

Creating a Cohesive Community Through Social Media

Pete Freeman
RECENT GRADUATE, NOBLESVILLE HIGH SCHOOL, NOBLESVILLE, INDIANA
AWARDED THE ELI-LILLY SCHOLARSHIP—A FULL SCHOLARSHIP TO
UNIVERSITY OF NOTRE DAME

I'm obsessed with the idea of sawdust.

Sawdust was worthless. People had to pay someone to take it away!

Then, at the turn of the nineteenth century, a factory worker decided to take leftover sawdust home. He used it to make particleboard, mulch, and charcoal briquettes. He died a millionaire, and, today, sawdust is a billion dollar industry. He took something valueless and brought value to it.

My vision as a student was to take something I was carrying around with very little value and give it life. I could've coasted and just checked out my senior year. Instead, I began the term by launching MillPulse.com, a website produced from all the "sawdust" of my first three years of high school. My team included a CTO [Chief Technology Officer] with a knack for video production, a COO [Chief Operations Officer] with political know-how beyond his years, and myself. I use the terms CTO and COO loosely. After all, my team members are my classmates and best friends, Harrison and David, without whom MillPulse.com would look like any other website before the first dot-com bubble burst. But let's get back to the sawdust.

I sat at my kitchen table on the first day of summer after junior year. This was it. I was going to make something special out of nothing. Sawdust, baby… sawdust.

I realized that, in three years at Noblesville High School, I'd met hundreds of teachers and thousands of students, or "millers." I was the editor of the high school newspaper and had my finger on the pulse of our school's culture.

I realized I could brand the NHS experience! By producing relevant, creative content, I could influence our student body and create positive change in our community. MillPulse was born.

And it was kept alive through social media. Just like a baby is born needing oxygen to breathe, so MillPulse needed social media. It is my organization's oxygen.

At the beginning of senior year, my team and I reached out to students through the MillPulse's Snapchat, Vine, Twitter, Instagram, and Facebook channels, as well as the website. The order in which I listed those is the order in which our student body was the most responsive to our content. (Thank you, big data.) With our audience in mind, we created content specific to each platform, storytelling around our high school's culture. Around Christmas, MillPulse had a returning audience of roughly 700 students.

Then what? Positive change! MillPulse set a school record for fundraising—$1,500.24 in less than two weeks. It could not have been done without our student body responding positively to the MillPulse brand and its messaging about the importance of supporting the Leukemia/Lymphoma Society through Pennies for Patients.

After the fundraiser, we maintained the momentum by launching the Miller Message campaign. Volunteers took Vine videos of students stating their messages. We heard everything from Bible verses to Wiz Khalifa lyrics! The videos were tweeted to our audience and cataloged on our website. Wouldn't it be neat to watch your co-worker or best friend share his most meaningful message with the world? We thought so, too. And because each is under six seconds, students are able to watch tens or hundreds of student messages in a cool ten minutes. Now *that's* the power of technology… from sawdust.

Following the fundraiser, the students behind MillPulse gained notoriety among the student body. Why stop with the MillPulse brand? Personal brand became the name of the game. All those pictures I had of me accepting state science fair awards, spending time with my gorgeous girlfriend, Victoria, and being presented the Eli-Lilly Endowment Scholarship became sawdust gold. I started storytelling. Pictures, quotes, videos, audio files, and jokes brought my friends even closer. Newspapers began covering me. I had a spot on television for a mentoring nonprofit I began. I was asked to speak to groups of students about owning their education.

I had become completely transparent; I was honest. I encouraged classmates to seize opportunities in, around and outside the classroom. Grades are no longer a measure of intellect. We live in an era where it has never been more disadvantageous to be fact smart. *Jeopardy!* winners are out. Innovators are in. EQ's worth is greater than IQ. The innovative empath trumps the methodical manager. These words can hurt, especially teachers. But complacency kills, and if I were going to live my life transparently in exchange for my own brand, I was going to be honest doing it. And all the while, my MillPulse sawdust soared in users and popularity.

"*I **encouraged classmates** to seize **opportunities** in, around and outside the classroom.*"
—**Pete Freeman**

The advice I give students? Start something with your sawdust and stand out. Your personal brand will follow, or even precede, if you have taken steps toward this innovation—and you will stand for a cause. Moreover, your teachers and peers will recognize your initiative. Don't forget, Rome wasn't built in a day. Likewise, merely pooling your sawdust into an innovative idea won't yield results. You have to execute, day after day.

Sure, having a good GPA is nice. But creating a brand from sawdust and executing on what you are most passionate about is the key to long-term success. Grades guarantee you good standing in your school. Executing on your sawdust guarantees you a promising career, an interesting life and personal influence that can be leveraged for progress and assistance.

At the end of my high school career, I reflected on all the people we'd highlighted, teachers we'd humanized, and stories we'd told. Lots of sawdust had come together, and, like particleboard, it created a cohesive whole from many unique, individual parts. By we, I mean MillPulse. Because, after all, if your brand isn't as human as possible, who wants to interact with it?

In the future, I want to give talks about students owning their education. I owned mine and came out with a gift much larger than my 4.0 GPA. I owe this experience to innovation, execution and to branding myself as I truly am.

And sawdust, baby. Lots of sawdust.

Hands-On Learning, Meeting a Need

Jake Ferrante and Christopher Woodle

FORMER STUDENTS, CAT NETWORK SYSTEMS ADMINISTRATOR
PROGRAM (CNSAP), LAKEWOOD HIGH SCHOOL'S CENTER FOR
ADVANCED TECHNOLOGIES, TAMPA, FLORIDA

> **Note:** *Both Jake and Christopher have the honor of being in Lou Zulli's class. Lou is a master teacher whom I met five years ago at a conference. He has been a mentor to me ever since. If you are interested in empowering your students with technology, I strongly suggest you connect with Mr. Zulli. Find him on Twitter: @lzulli.*

For many, the CAT Network Systems Administrator Program (CN-SAP) at Lakewood High School's Center for Advanced Technologies is a portal into the vast world of computer science. Headed by Mr. Lou Zulli, the CNSAP program provides students with hands-on, engaging, real-work experience as one would expect in a professional work setting. Handing us the tools to our success upon entering the door, Mr. Zulli's open-learning approach provides students who have a propensity for information technology or programming with the opportunity to grow at their own pace and to explore what works best for them. In the end, it is up to us whether we take advantage of this amazing opportunity.

In a place where critical thinking is the norm, one philosophy to live by is that great problem solvers ask great questions. So, when we were invited to get involved in the development of the Madeira Beach project, we instantly began asking crucial questions like these:

- How would a professional do it? We wanted to approach the situation in the same manner as someone with years of experience would.

- What are the needs of the customer? We knew that determining the needs of the customer is a key element in deciding the framework on which the project will be built.

- Am I asking the right question? This was the most important question to keep in our minds when dealing with a problem. The rule: If you're stuck hitting walls left and right, rethink your question.

One of the many questions that were asked in the beginning of this project was: What is the right way to accomplish this task?

The request made to us was to make a website for a school, Madeira Beach Fundamental. The parameters included creating a working content management system that is simple enough for anyone to operate, yet upholds industry standard security requirements to handle student and faculty information as well as insure the integrity of the site. Since neither of us ever had tackled a project on this scale before, we needed to do some research to determine which architectural model would work best. Narrowing down our research, we discovered the potential hidden in ASP.NET framework. Deciding the right data structure was central in determining the direction in this project. Once we had in mind what model would fit our needs, we were able to start tearing apart example projects and learning anything and everything we could about how components worked and shape them to better fit the project's intended outcome.

Transitioning from designing static web pages with some dynamic JavaScript content to using active server pages presented a huge learning curve. We did this by implementing C# with Razor, a syntax used to create dynamic web pages with C# and Visual Basic, into our HTML pages. Our prior years in the CAT program gave us some background knowledge pertaining to object-oriented programming, but learning how to deploy a solution with server-side code to handle information in a safe and secure manner was definitely a challenge. After decompiling and investigating how example templates worked, we were able to create our own back-end solution, custom tailored to fit the needs of the project. This process was an essential and most challenging part of the project, and, unquestionably, required the most attention to detail.

> *"In the end, this was an enormous project, and **we are proud** to say we tackled it. It was no easy task, but it was **well worth the effort.**"*
>
> *—Jake Ferrante and Christopher Woodle*

Part of learning how to become efficient at programming is learning how to use the tools at your disposal. A few of the tools we needed to learn how to use included Visual Studio and our own development SQL databases. Becoming acquainted with these tools can take some time, and that was not something we had a lot of. While learning the model-view-controller (MVC) framework, we also spent time learning the ins and outs of how to use Team Foundation Server, a cloud storage system for Visual Studio Projects, as well as numerous SQL database tools and complimentary tools that come alone with Visual Studio.

As busy students always working at school, home and on the go, we needed a way to access our code from anywhere. Team Foundation Server (TFS), a cloud service that works in conjunction with Visual Studio to host projects online, was an indispensable component to the completion of this project. Whether we were working at school side-by-side or if one of us was out grabbing coffee and needed to quickly jump online, we were able to sign in and edit our code on the go. It didn't matter where we were or what we were doing, if either of us came up with an idea for the project, we were able to quickly access our code and upload it to the cloud. This made it extremely easy for us to communicate and upload different versions of the project. Having access to previous versions of our project created somewhat of a safety net and allowed us to experiment with our methods without risking data loss.

Another tremendous feat that we accomplished was figuring how to use IIS, configure SQL and use tools pertaining to SQL databases, especially SQL management tools built into Visual Studio. Mastering these tools was imperative to implementing features that were key components in this project, like handling database information from the faculty control panel. We were able to use tools available in Visual Studio to manage our database schemas, publish our project to our development server, as well as debug our solution right on our own computer.

The single most important aspect of this project was creating a solution that not only fit the needs of the end user, but making something that could be used again and again—something that the user would enjoy going back to when they needed to complete a task. To do this, we needed to take a step back and approach the problem from another angle. We needed to become the consumer. We started asking questions: How would someone use this product? How effective is this product at completing the task at hand? What features hold the most importance? By asking these questions, we were able to design not only an aesthetically pleasing product but also a product optimized and streamlined to fit the needs of the customer. There is an old saying: Form follows function. In CAT, we have a different perspective: Form equals function.

Although the Madeira Beach project had many challenges, we were able to take away valuable information from it like no other project we had ever attempted before. We learned better code practices, ended up creating our own styling frameworks and implemented several languages to create a single product. Migrating what was once client-side code to be handled server-side was a huge step towards optimizing the user experience. Developing with the ASP.NET framework gave us a better understanding of file management, as well as code efficiency. We were able to instantiate a file upload system for administrators to upload faculty photos and newsletters using native ASP.NET functionality to keep code consolidated. And most of all, working as a team, we honed our communication and time management skills. If we needed something done, we talked about it, and set a deadline.

In the end, this was an enormous project, and we are proud to say we tackled it. It was no easy task, but it was well worth the effort. The amount of knowledge and understanding of new ways of programming gained from this experience has left us ready and eager to take on whatever lies ahead.

Learning how to Fail

Madeleine Clark

FORMER BROADCASTING STUDENT, FRANKLIN COMMUNITY HIGH SCHOOL RECENT GRADUATE, DUKE UNIVERSITY, RECEIVED A FULL SCHOLARSHIP TO DUKE UNIVERSITY

You know what no one ever says? "Failing is fun!"

The powerful notions of learn from your mistakes, it's not the destination but the journey, and everything is as it should be exist in almost every culture. From the airy English, *If at first you don't succeed!* to the delightfully Russian, *The first pancake is always a blob*, the idea is a familiar one.

But hand-in-hand with these nugget-sized aphorisms come gloomy words like struggle, perseverance, pain, and failure. Even courage and grit are kind of somber. I mean, Sisyphus's day-to-day life wasn't super fun and eating a blobby pancake isn't particularly enjoyable.

The turning-failure-into-success movement has recently gained even more momentum with the explosion of entrepreneurship and start-up culture. Megan McArdle's beautiful book, *The Up Side of Down,* gives compelling, relatable advice about how to fail well. It draws on the experiences of founders from Steve Jobs to Colonel Sanders, to show how failure is often the single most important factor in later success. But even though the tone of her book is overall optimistic, she probably wouldn't go so far as to tell a classroom full of hopeful high schoolers that failure is fun.

But, you know, sometimes it totally is. And whether or not we can appreciate that, failure and our response to it is what defines us.

Going into university, I had never experienced anything remotely close to failure. Much like any child who is pre-selected by the nefarious primary school routine of test, excel, be showered with praise, rinse, repeat as a good student, the first eighteen years of my life were almost perfectly formulaic and full of gold stars. I rose at six, ate a good breakfast, studied, excelled in class, arrived promptly to afternoon dance/sports/academic club practices (participation in all of which was, I was told, a nonnegotiable requirement of someday getting into a good school), finished my homework, and got approximately 8 hours of sleep every night.

The rigidity of my personal routine was paralleled perfectly in the course of my academic life. Go to class, ace the tests, score a seat in the accelerated subjects, prep for those spirit-killing, academic hurdles students must clear to prove their merit to universities and, finally, finally receive that piece of parchment paper, preferably from an Ivy League or an equivalently rigorous program that promises a successful future.

I did these things. My GPA was fantastic, I was an All-State athlete, and I was constantly showered with awards. For my talents, I was rewarded with scholarships to a top-ten university, where I went on to complete double majors and rack up quite a nice resume of activities and awards.

So to reiterate: I never failed at anything before I went to university. I was the high school senior who still went home in tears over a grade of A minus.

And then, I went to Duke University. And suddenly, I wasn't the top. In fact, I was failing—all the time. And most of those failures weren't particularly fun.

Over the course of my four years at college, I went through a series of failures that made me wonder if I was even qualified to be a human being, let alone one who was taking up a spot in a prestigious university that could have been filled with someone else, someone more deserving. I was flatly rejected from participating in a service project that's considered to be "literally the best thing about Duke, ever." I had a series of disastrous relationships, both platonic and romantic. I handled my parents' divorce badly, and let my anger overwhelm an entire semester. As a junior, I failed (yes, with an F) an introductory statistics class that was meant for underclassmen. I completely ruined part of a professor's research. I didn't finish my thesis in time.

Those were the pain, struggle, and perseverance examples of failing. And don't get me wrong, each of those was immensely educational and I grew personally and professionally with each one. I learned how to study properly, to understand that rejection is a natural part of life and not to take it personally, to treat those around me with better empathy and to improve how I dealt with emotional stress. I gained the experience that helped me grow into a more grounded, wholesome person, and could write any number of pithy little self-help books about all the great things I took away from each rough patch.

But man, those lessons, while valuable, were absolutely in no way fun. My next batch of pancakes have, so far, come out much smoother, but that first blobby one was pretty repulsive.

You know what, though? All those painful, gritty failures are completely outshined an experience that showed me can failing be fun and that the best parts of your life can be a series of otherwise pretty ambiguous failures.

Sophomore year, I joined an incubator for young entrepreneurs called InCube and learned to fail brilliantly, beautifully, outrageously, and, all the while, had the absolutely best time of my life.

The eighteen students who made up InCube's first class were part of a brand-new endeavor by a group of passionate, ultra-effective upperclassmen to bolster a fledgling university innovation and entrepreneurship campaign. We were a living community where members shared apartment buildings, workspace, and access to funding and mentorship and were encouraged to bring our very diverse talents together and collaborate on business ventures.

The first year, we turned out six new companies and a handful of apps, some of which went on to achieve great success. Most of these startups were the collaborative efforts of multiple InCubers. More importantly, however, we turned out probably a hundred or more ideas and companies that went absolutely nowhere.

> "We chose the startup life **because we loved it**, not to get a little gold star on our college careers."
> —**Madeleine Clark**

Actually, we failed at a lot of things—even the logistics of keeping a community together. We had an attrition rate of over 50 percent at the turn of the year. It took us the better part of six months to even finalize a specific, codified vision for the organization and, after a 12-hour marathon meeting that wasn't allowed to end until we wrote a constitution, a lot of us left the common room feeling disheartened and, in some cases, offended. Some of us never came back after that.

We fought, reconciled, compromised, persuaded, and sulked. Companies succeeded, and the rest of us were a little jealous; and companies failed, and we empathized. Friends and co-founders found each other and, sometimes, split.

But what we had going for us more than anything was our cultural dedication to Work Hard, Play Hard. While we were forming LLCs and networking and slogging away at soul-crushing code, we were caught up in extreme games of FIFA and nights out at laser tag. We were kids, and we had a great time together. And somehow, in the midst of all this, a handful of teens and twenty-somethings were able to examine the very foundations of innovation, entrepreneurship, and education.

My year with InCube was the best of my life. And I didn't succeed with a single idea. Some of them were embarrassingly bad, actually, and I was totally unprepared to enter the startup world. My first startup idea was a print newspaper (Ha!). I hated coding and felt like a complete fool every time I tried to learn it; the sixth lesson of CodeAcademy may have just been assigning names to things, but it had me ready to chuck my computer off the balcony. I chose not to re-apply to InCube for the following year because academic pressures were far too high. My Zen wasn't strong enough to allow myself to fail out of college and be okay with it. I lost some friends.

But those failures were so, so incredibly fun. It wasn't just that we were having fun outside of the community; it's that the entire culture was dedicated to the pursuit of fun. We chose the startup life because we loved it, not to get a little gold star on our college careers.

There's nothing quite like the feeling of investing 50, 100, or 3,000 hours into a project only to realize, at the end of the year, that it's never, ever going to get off the ground, let alone make you Zuckerberg billions. Just when I'd burnt myself out so entirely I thought I was going to fail out of life forever and end up broke, friendless, and living out of my parents' shed, someone else in InCube failed. And someone else. And someone else. And these someones were my friends.

And then someone succeeded, but maybe their definition of success was just finally debugging one tenth of their code, maybe it was finally getting their first $50,000 sponsorship. And then maybe I succeeded, by convincing a tough crowd that computer science majors aren't the only valuable innovators or by impressing a donor enough to give us more money for the coming year.

And thanks to this lovely balance of abject failure and enthusiastic success, we all realized we were in the same boat, working for the same thing and that we all came out of InCube knowing a little about what it takes to succeed and a whole lot more about what it doesn't.

So we all went into post-grad life swinging. We saw that a ragtag group of hackers, dreamers, and talkers could do something amazing and tell people about it. We saw that business and fun shouldn't be separated. We saw that we could do great things with brilliant people, who also happened to be friends.

That was an education. We failed, and we had fun.

It was the journey, not the destination. Everything was as it should be. We took our blobby pancakes and smothered them in chocolate sauce and those garish rainbow sprinkles, and they were delicious.

Moving Forward

I **hope** this journey has sparked some ideas for innovative projects your class can start. Most importantly, I hope you find the joy of taking on Innovation Class or Genius Hour projects that lead to new discoveries—for you and your students.

Where do you go from here? How do you take that first step? Moving forward comes down to three practices: giving yourself permission, transparency, and trust.

Give Yourself Permission

A former student taught me an important lesson about permission. He came in to see me after school, and, with a grin, handed me a business card. It read: Chad Smith, CEO Green Clean Lawn Service. The seventeen-year-old explained that he had always wanted to be the CEO of a company. He'd taken to heart my mantra, "When you treat yourself like a professional, people will do the same." Because he had mown a few lawns in his neighborhood the previous summer, he thought he would take things a step further that summer and be a company. He printed up a few business cards, and *voilà*, Chad was the CEO of his very own company! Did he hire a lawyer or conduct a copyright search for his company name? Did he have a degree in business? Did he have any employees? No. He hadn't even purchased a mower yet. But he had given himself permission to be a professional. His self-appointed title made him feel powerful. And from what I hear, his landscape venture went very well that season.

I'm asking you to give yourself permission to innovate—to change the way you teach, learn, and collaborate. You don't need to ask if you can do something innovative in your classroom. You don't need to be a "tech" teacher to be an innovator or need an Innovation Class to start engaging in student-led projects. But you do need to give yourself a title change. Whether you teach math, social studies, language arts, science, you are a teacher of *innovation* because you choose to look at education differently.

Allowing students choice and being willing to let them work with outside mentors is innovative. Plant your flag into the ground and stake your claim: You are an innovative educator—one who incorporates new, exciting lessons and looks for collaborative opportunities for your students. An innovative educator does not simply teach a topic but rather finds sources to enhance the classroom experience through technology, mentors, travel, and by doing things differently. As an innovative educator, you will play several roles: **Project Manager**, **Public Relations Manager**, **Travel Agent**, and **Venture Capitalist.**

PROJECT MANAGER

Every great project needs some oversight and guidance from the teacher. While these projects are student-led, a good project manager (the teacher) helps students make decisions along the way. This is not to say you should manage the entire project or set up their calendar, but a good manager asks probing questions and challenges students to think deeper. Remember, learning in an innovative environment is not about seeking validation but, rather, navigating and solving problems. A project manager can offer feedback, which is a nice way of saying criticism—a vital ingredient to growth. A great project manager also knows how to network and connect students to other experts. Pointing them toward your network helps them, but make your students responsible for contacting experts and potential mentors. After all, Obi-Wan did not train Luke in the ways of the Force, but directed him toward opportunities and other mentors that allowed him to grow. (Sorry, my inner Star Wars geek came out.)

> **You** are a teacher of innovation because you **choose to look at education differently**.

PUBLIC RELATIONS / MEDIA RELATIONS MANAGER

Using the bullhorn of social media is one way, of many, that a teacher becomes a good public relations manager. And remember, local newspapers and television stations need good news. *Nothing* beats a feel-good story about local students doing amazing work. You have power in getting the local media to pay attention to what your students are doing. Rather than complaining about the negative media coverage of education today, get proactive and give the newsmen something positive to report. They will support you! Put on your press relations hat and call the local paper. Tell them about your students' projects. Let the television station know that your class is collaborating with a newsworthy mentor and embarking on a learning journey. They will *eat it up*! However, I must warn you that you should be doing something that is actually innovative. Inviting a reporter into a classroom to see new innovative poster boards from the whale unit won't cut it. Getting an oceanographer to do a live Skype call while on location might get them in.

Travel Agent

As a kid, I got to travel a lot every summer. My dad was in education and my mom was a stay-at-home mom—also making her an educator. They made an effort for our family to travel. Because we were on a budget, we traveled by truck and pop-up camper. I have vivid memories of camping. What I really appreciate now is all the knowledge I picked up along the way. Our travel wasn't educational in the traditional sense, although we did visit almost every National Park in the country. Traveling gave me a chance to learn something new, to experience different cultures, taste new foods, and meet new friends at every new Jellystone Park™ or KOA® campground along our journey. Seeing and trying new things as a child permanently engaged my sense of curiosity—something that serves me well today.

Traveling is an important part of education. It gives students the opportunity to see things through a different lens. And when they return home, their perspective has changed.

Grant Litchman used to head up an annual trip to the Philippines for Francis Parker School in San Diego. "I loved taking the students there because it was *not* a vacation," he told me. "I wanted them to see how many people live on less than $2 a day. The trip provided a perspective that they cannot get from a textbook. But more importantly, the trip created lasting friendships and understanding." Litchman explained that collaboration opportunities often developed when the students returned to the states. "Some of the students went on to create awareness campaigns; some tried to raise funds for organizations or causes that they connected with on the trip."

That's what I love about Litchman's trips—the experience created a new understanding about the world and provided ongoing collaboration opportunities. When students go to a place like the Philippines, everything is new to them. The perspective gained by going to another location allows them to see different possibilities. Collaboration from that point forward is often more authentic.

Now, maybe you're thinking, "What if you have a budget of $0? What type of traveling can you do then?" That's okay, because travel can include going to the next hallway, across town, or even taking a virtual trip. Traveling can be as easy as taking your class out into the school courtyard, or even the room for the next grade level up. Having a fourth grade class observe what is different in the fifth grade hallway can produce all sorts of fun observations. Many teachers enjoy spontaneously taking a class outside to read on a nice day;

> Be on the lookout for **opportunities beyond the classroom** to enhance your students' **insight, creativity,** and **collaboration** prospects.

it spurs the students' creativity and is just plain fun. Taking a quick day trip somewhere in town is usually cheap and inexpensive. And joining a virtual tour is not too difficult, especially with good 4G cell phone signals and a willingness to ask around for virtual tour guides. Andrew Vanden Heuvel, one of the first educators to use Google Glass, decided to take a tour of the CERN particle accelerator near Geneva, Switzerland. As he toured the facility, a class full of science students came along with him, virtually, as his glass camera live streamed the entire event! A class in Michigan couldn't afford to fly to Europe, but a virtual tour worked nicely. During the tour, the students met the scientists who worked there and made connections with future collaborators!

Playing the travel agent role well means that you must be on the lookout for opportunities beyond the classroom to enhance your students' insight, creativity, and collaboration prospects. Whether you arrange for your class to travel to another country or just take time to discover some other part of the school building, travel is always worth the effort.

Venture Capitalist

Innovation projects sometimes need some money to get off the ground. So, what is an innovative educator to do when budgets are tight? The first, and usually most effective, method to find money is asking around your local community. You'll have greater success if you are enthusiastic and passionate about your students' projects. Local business leaders and parents want to support proactive, highly visible projects. Let them know why the project is important and remind them that it is a student-led initiative. Remember, not unlike sponsoring team shirts for youth sports leagues, this is an opportunity for the business leaders to show their good will. Putting their logo on the back of a shirt demonstrates that the business cares about the community. In the same way, when you are promoting a highly visible project, like starting a community garden, several businesses might want to get on the class project bandwagon. It's a win for the school and the business that receives positive press!

Local support is always best. When that doesn't bring in enough, you may want to use a crowdfunding site. I have personally used and supported projects through edbacker.com, gofundme.com, donorschoose.org, and kickstarter.com, and found that these can be useful. I've even seen a few unique crowdfunding campaigns go viral. Uniqueness and innovation are essential to successful crowdfunding campaigns. Raising funds to buy a tablet isn't likely to draw nearly as much traffic as asking people to help start a book exchange to Kenya. Remember, the media, your social media networks, and your local community *want* to support your class. Make sure they know what you are doing! Get out there, be visible, and raise those funds!

Transparency

Accountability is a sore subject with some educators and union reps who are exasperated by administrators (and politicians) who want to monitor what is going on in the classroom. The days of shutting the door and teaching what you want to teach are, for better or worse, over. A uniform standard across the profession seems to be the continuing norm. Unfortunately, some of the standards, which set the bar to cover minimum skills, may be holding really creative teachers back. For the go-get-'em teacher who covers the standards and wants to move past the minimum, transparency is vital. In fact, being transparent in our classrooms is one of the most vital and innovative things we can do. By teaching for the world to see, innovative educators quiet the critics and demonstrate best practices for other teachers.

The twenty-first century skills of critical thinking, communication, collaboration, and creativity are essential to moving our students forward. Providing a class that embraces these skills, while allowing opportunities for real-world collaboration with the outside world *and* being transparent, will change not only the students' lives, but also hearts, minds, and policies of those calling the shots in education today.

My challenge is for teachers to take the attitude that it's better to ask for forgiveness than permission. Commit to covering the standards for compliance and be equally committed to ensuring that your students are empowered and equipped for real life. Innovation Classes and Genius Hours may be out of the norm but, once you get going, and, by the time any non-supporting administration figures out that you're doing something different, the projects and student commitment will speak for itself. Not once have I heard complaints about my students collaborating with universities. The community never claimed that we should do more memorization work and focus less on networking with mentors. In fact, you might be surprised by how supportive your school's administration becomes when they see your students' engagement. Parents will see enthusiasm on their child's face and feel the passion they have for their projects. Key community members will want to hop on board, and politicians might even want to take some of the credit. Once they see the undeniable proof of your class's success, your administration will start supporting you.

Professional Jealousy

A more difficult issue might be convincing other teachers to get on board. I must admit this is where I made a huge error in my former position. I created my own little niche of innovation and kept it to myself. I let the collaboration come from outside the school building and didn't think to look within. I didn't make an effort to involve other teachers at school because I was chasing "cool" opportunities outside my state. Eventually, the success created some jealousy and rightfully so. The local paper and even television news programs regularly featured our Innovation and Broadcasting classes. I knew how to wear that media relations hat and did so often. I wanted to create great stories for all of my students… my students. I should have been working harder to find innovative opportunities to help serve in the other classrooms and collaborate with them as well.

Thankfully, I learned from my mistake of being too focused on my classroom. I recently took a position at another school as an Innovation Coordinator. Although I still run some Innovation Classes, I also provide support and guidance for other teachers. Much like a technology coach, I am now working with teachers to create great opportunities and learning adventures. I've learned that, for real success, collaboration must come from outside *and* inside our school.

In talking to many other innovation educators, I know professional jealousy can and does occur. Some of your fellow teachers may feel they are being shown up. Some may be resentful because the success of your projects will force them into trying the same things. This can be a real problem. The solution, I believe, is to remain enthusiastic and be willing to work *with* other teachers. Doing so opens up the lines of communication and allows true collaboration to begin.

> The **spark** that an **innovative educator** provides can **change the school culture.**

As you set up a culture of innovation for your students, pause to consider how you can create a culture of innovation within your professional community. The teacher who goes rogue and doesn't extend the invitation to take the innovation journey might be in for a short, tense ride. Here's the reality: Innovation projects can and will fail from time to time. If you've alienated your colleagues by not inviting them in your journey, it's very likely that they will celebrate your mistakes when some of the projects fall flat.

However, if you successfully create a team atmosphere that is inviting and transparent, opportunities and cooperation will multiply. I have seen entire schools rally around and be transformed by projects. The spark that an innovative educator provides *can* change the school culture. Just give it time; Rome wasn't built in a day. So please, find the happy balance between the superstar teacher, who is a bit of a showoff, and the quiet, unassuming teacher who doesn't want to make waves. The showoff will not have the support of the teachers, and the shy teacher cannot get the message out to the community members.

Trust

Finally, you need trust. This journey has allowed me to connect with hundreds of inspired, innovative educators. It doesn't matter if they teach third-grade math, middle-school science, or high-school calculus, innovation is an attitude that is fostered by a community of trust. If you go to a school that is known for its best practices, you can bet that the administration trusts its teachers. Forward-thinking administrators look beyond the check list and replace the top down mentality with a grassroots, student-centered approach. This cannot happen unless the school administration extends trust to the teachers and students.

Former Milford High School Principal, Eric Sheninger, routinely shines a spotlight on what teachers and students are doing in class. He asks them to use social media to drive traffic to the authentic student work and even encourages them to spark discussion on social media throughout the day!

Yes, he expects students to live tweet class discussions. He urges teachers to post important events on the Facebook site. Could this experiment with social media and transparency come back to bite him? Maybe… but it hasn't. Instead, the students and teachers he's worked with have taken his trust and run with it. These students know about digital citizenship because of trust and high expectations.

Eric Williams, a superintendent in Virginia, says, "We encourage the students to get out their cell phones and utilize them as learning tools, and we support the teachers who try this approach. The biggest issue has been fear." For this approach to education to work, the district's school networks allow students to access sites like Twitter and YouTube.

Williams explains that extending trust helps students learn how to use and respect technology. "We have a student-driver approach where the students are behind the wheel. We know that the students are going to make some mistakes down the road, but we want the teacher there as coach," he says. "We know the students are going to use cell phone technology, so we might as well be the coach to show them how to use it responsibly and empower them for showcasing their knowledge."

Both Sheninger and Williams are leaders that get it. They know students and teachers might make mistakes. They determine boundaries and create a culture and tone of trust over fear—and it's working.

quick thoughts

- Give yourself permission to be an innovator.

- Innovators have many job descriptions, including: Project Manager, Media Relations Manager, Travel Agent, and Venture Capitalist.

- Being transparent provides greater collaboration and encourages students and teachers to push past the minimum standards.

- Include as many teachers as you can to sidestep professional jealousy.

- Trust must be at the heart of any classroom. Administrators need to understand that teachers and students are going to make some mistakes and must trust that they will conduct themselves with professionalism.

notes

Coming Together:
Speaking the Same Language

**"There's something happening here.
What it is ain't exactly clear."**
—Buffalo Springfield, "For What It's Worth"

Genius Hour	Maker Space
20% Time	Tinker Time
Google Time	Hacked Learning
Passion time	Innovation Class

The terms we educators use to explain how we're incorporating innovative learning techniques into the classroom aren't always clear to the outside world or even to other educators. Still, no matter the terms we use, a common goal drives the brave efforts we employ to get our students fully engaged, and, more importantly, to take ownership of their learning experience. And our efforts point to the same reality: Increased student engagement that allows greater freedom and trial-and-error learning addresses the needs of our new world.

Dr. David Preston of Ernest Righetti High School in Santa Maria, California, brings yet another term to the table. I was introduced to Preston (@prestonlearning) through Howard Rheingold at Stanford who had interviewed us both for his blog, *DML Central.* Howard's site is dedicated to looking at ways to use digital media in education as well as how to improve learning through the power of collaboration and participation.

I was immediately impressed by the passion and purpose with which Preston works. After working as a management consultant and teaching at UCLA for eleven years, he came to believe that the best place to reform education was *before* students reached the university level. So, he became a high school English teacher. And like me, Preston wants students to get connected and learn from multiple sources of media, people, and experiences. He calls this type of education *Open Source Learning (OSL).*

Open Source Learning

After working with Preston, I believe that OSL aptly describes the goals of all the different terms we use to define innovative education. OSL means to find any source of information to help empower the learner. Students might consult an encyclopedia, a person, mentors, or other course curricula. OSL is a comprehensive term that teachers can use to describe any project in any subject. For example: "In health class, we will be doing an OSL project on the effects of weight gain from the switch to four passing periods of block scheduling from the regular seven passing periods." Or, "In Social Studies, we will be doing an OSL project by identifying local landmarks and learning the stories of their significance to the town by connecting with local residents." You see my point; OSL has a nice, comprehensive sound to it. It's a good place to start if you are looking to incorporate some innovative techniques in your classroom. Likewise, it's a simple but comprehensive term that may help us all—educators and students–to speak the same language. According to Preston, OSL is about creating the conditions that favor personalized learning; we can all agree to basic principles and still do things in very different, innovative ways.

Open Source can also mean that the OSL class itself can be used as an example, just like open source code software. Collaborative sites, like Reddit.com, have been open source, and some of the best innovations on that site were transformed by hackers (the good kind) who brought improvements to Reddit's open

OSL *means to find* **any** *source of* **information** *to* *help* **empower** *the learner.*

code. I often remind my students that the projects they are working on might inspire other students around the world. That knowledge pushes them to work harder and master their subjects. The reminder that they are an example for others helps them make the mental, and actual, shift from being a consumer of knowledge to a content producer.

Whatever term you use to describe what happens in your class, I hope you've been inspired by this book to integrate innovation into every class period and every subject. Personally, I would like to see more schools add an Innovation Class to their course titles. I mentioned before that my Innovation Class uses the catalog title Group Discussions, a Language Arts elective; but what about teachers who teach science or math? With the emphasis on STEM (Science, Technology, Engineering, Math) and STEAM (STEM + Art), educators from math and science could offer relevant Innovation Classes that could open up tremendous opportunities for collaboration and enhance the math or science curriculum. When encouraged to harness their passions and to apply these core subjects to today's problems and needs, the creations and discoveries that could result from students' imagination and expert collaborations are unlimited.

Innovate Now

It may take some years before most schools dare to offer entire classes dedicated to innovation. That is why I wrote this book: I wanted to set the vision for what is possible and start a dialogue to move things forward. I also wanted to encourage all educators to incorporate more innovation and collaboration into our curriculum, *now*. That's why so much of this book focuses on the fact that teachers need to be innovators first; it is imperative that we model these behaviors for our students. Don't wait for your school's administration to catch on. The students who are taking your courses need to know how to think for themselves. They need to know how to discover their passions, work with others, behave like professionals, and use social media effectively and appropriately. Even without a course description titled *Innovation Class,* you can impart those skills and help your students build character traits that will serve them well. And if you are a student or parent, my advice to you is to find your own opportunities to innovate. The point is, you don't really need a formal classroom to change the world. If you attend a school that won't embrace innovation and collaboration, please don't wait around for them. Create your own path.

I get a lot of questions about whether a separate Innovation Class would be valuable for the elementary levels. While it would be great, it isn't necessary. I believe a Genius Hour approach is best in the early grades, but I also encourage teachers to go beyond an hour of innovation. There are hundreds of successful examples of awesome work being done by grades K-8. I've pointed out a few in previous chapters. Students in kindergarten through third grade are particularly adept at taking risks. They thrive when given a chance to discover their passion. Students seem to lose some of their enthusiasm and passion for learning when they reach upper elementary and middle levels. By high school, it seems they are mired in SAT scores, AP classes, and GPA contests. That's why encouraging the Genius Hour, or whatever term you choose to call it, at younger levels works well. It maximizes their natural

> **You** *don't really need a formal classroom to* **change the world. Create your own path.**

curiosity and love for learning and prepares them for innovation at the upper levels. The hope is that, by the time our students enter high school or even middle school, they have been trained how to look for opportunities and collaborate with experts. Then, they will be able to craft a vibrant brand to showcase the awesome work they create. The education system must do a better job of encouraging innovation—taking risks and fostering passion through learning—if we want to equip our students for the real world. If we start this culture of innovation early and support students all the way through their high school years, I firmly believe that they will be better prepared for college and become true agents of change as *innovators*!

Lastly, educators need to band together and show the world that education is moving in the right direction. Being transparent and media savvy will demonstrate that education is moving forward and adapting to the changing landscape of what a school is designed to provide. We can transform our schools into a hub of collaborative learning, where the students can learn from sources all over the world. Our schools' missions can change from providing subservient factory workers to free thinkers, who can create new concepts or products that can change the way we live!

I am optimistic that education can pivot to this type of innovation model. Heck, I'm optimistic that our politicians can change and adopt some innovation and transparency, too! The education revolution is already underway, but more educators need to start talking the same language, draw on the courage of community, and gain strength by working together. Eventually, transformation will come. While that's in the works, be bold enough to take risks, allow the classroom to seem messy, and get good at improving as you grow and learn *with* your students.

I would love to hear from you! You can always contact me on Twitter: @donwettrick, or email me at: dwettrick@gmail.com. I am passionate about what I do, and will make every attempt to help any student, educator, or parent who asks. My blog, theinnovationteacher.com, provides resources for innovation in education, as well as ongoing updates from me and from other teachers who are committed to innovative learning. If you are an educator who works in a system where innovation and change are not welcome, please connect with me. I will try to help in any way I can to support you as you move forward.

Thank you for reading *Pure Genius*. Innovation is my mission. I hope you'll join me in the journey.

Opportunities Are Everywhere!
—Don Wettrick

notes

notes

Additional Resources

For more inspiration and information regarding education, innovation, and creativity, I recommend the following.

GREAT BOOKS TO READ

Drive by Daniel Pink
InGenius by Tina Seelig
Creating Innovators by Tony Wagner
Think Like a Freak by Steven Levitt and Stephen Dubner
Creative Confidence by Tom Kelley and David Kelley
Linchpin by Seth Godin
Teach Like a Pirate by Dave Burgess
Digital Leadership by Eric Sheninger
Out of Our Minds by Ken Robinson
How Children Succeed by Paul Tough
The Myths of Creativity by David Burkus
Creativity, Inc. by Ed Catmull and Amy Wallace

GREAT BLOGS TO FOLLOW

Edutopia.org
Teachthought.com
CoolCatTeacher.com
Gettingsmart.com
kqed.org/Mindshift
Kleinspiration.com
Twoguysandsomeipads.com
Edsurge.com
Innovativeteacher.org
Insidehighered.com
Learning.blogs.nytimes.com
Edudemic.com

About the Author

Don Wettrick is an Innovation Specialist at Noblesville High School, just outside Indianapolis, Indiana. Wettrick has served in education for the past sixteen years, teaching middle school and high school classes. Additionally, he is an educational and innovation consultant and speaker. He is passionate about helping students find their educational opportunities and providing them with the digital tools they need to give them a competitive edge.

Wettrick has lectured across the United States and Europe about collaboration, social media use, and environments that enable innovation. He also hosts an internet radio program, *InnovatED*, for the BAM! Radio Network. Most importantly, he works with educators and students to bring innovation and collaborative skills into education.

Wettrick lives in Indianapolis with his wife, Alicia, and three children, Ava, Anna, and Grant. You can find him on Twitter @donwettrick, where he tweets updates on his students' innovative work, and on his website theinnovationteacher.com.